REAL ES INVESTING 101

BY

CHAD MALONE

You agree that by continuing to read this book, where appropriate and/or necessary, you shall consult a professional (including but not limited to your doctor, attorney, or financial advisor or such other advisor as needed) before using any of the suggested remedies, techniques, or information in this book.

Table of Contents

INTRODUCTION

Like many people out there, you're probably looking for that one financial solution that ends all your money problems and frustration, am I right?

Of course, I am! But we know that making money outside of a job is a daunting task and a headache for most.

Coming up with an idea of what to do can be one of the hardest parts of starting up a business, and let's face it, we've got a very slim chance of starting the next Facebook or Uber.

So here we are. It's the property game, one of the most lucrative, sustainable business models out there that have made the most millionaires in history and also one of the very few that have the best blueprint to follow with regard to creating wealth in a step by step format.

I know it's scary. It was very scary for me too, especially at the beginning. But aren't all kinds of business?

Especially if you don't have previous experience or education relevant to this industry.

This is normal especially due to the fact that while real estate investment can be an extremely lucrative business no matter how old you are, it normally requires lots of time commitment and of course, a huge amount of money — or extremely good credit — just to get started. If you happen to be a busy millennial with not a lot of cash to spare, then a real estate investment trust or REIT might be a good place for you to start. But there are also many other alternatives.

Now, let's go back to the most important question to answer when investing in real estate… *can you afford it?*

I said "the most important" because it's an expensive endeavour to dive into, so looking into your budget should be a priority. Unless you have a lot of money laying around, you'll probably need to take alternative options for getting started with your investment. Investing in real estate is definitely a serious commitment, and your financial capability controls your ability to run this business.

Another question that you need to answer is… why?

You have to really understand your purpose as to why you want to invest in the real estate business. If you're investing to meet the needs of your family, then it would be smart to look at the land's papers and formalities like electricity, water, and the road connectivity to the estate. The location's proximity to shops, schools, and other establishments are some of the other things you must consider. If you're investing in a house that you're planning to turn into a home, then you must put a great consideration to the home's interior to see the extent of repairs that are necessary to make it comfortable to live in for you and your family.

If you're buying the estate exclusively for the purpose of reselling later on, then you must do more research on your choice of investment. You need to be aware of how much of an appreciation the land goes through and also analyse which areas are the ones that are going to bring you a return on investment. This is important as you don't want to put all your investment money on something that may not sell.

These points are only two of the important things you must consider when you want to invest in real estate – there are other important things you must know to be successful at it.

In this book, I'm going to give you a walkthrough on everything you need to know when investing in real estate and how to go about it to attain success in it.

Chapter 1

WHY INVEST IN REAL ESTATE?

The idea might just randomly come into your mind, or perhaps it's something that has always been bugging your mind. It might be a thoughtful little passing fantasy about purchasing that small seemingly abandoned house down the road and renovating it to sell for a profit. Or perhaps, you have considered buying a rental property and get rent to cover the mortgage. Regardless of how the idea formed in your mind, the important thing is that you've taken the step to learn how the world of real estate investment works.

Now, you know your personal reason… but the question is that, why is it a good idea?

The answer is that there is exceptional potential for revenue in real estate investment.

Investing in real estate is a sure-fire way of generating money and boosting your net worth. The money you make will likely depend on your knowledge, dedication, and game plan. There's no magic formula when it comes to real estate investment. Regardless of how simple the late-night millionaire's club makes this business seem, it wouldn't make you get rich overnight. It may take months and months before you can even buy a property, then more before you can sell one, and long before you can get a steady, comfortable revenue.

So, with the long process involved in this business, is it really worth it?

To put it simply, this IS a career option with potential revenue whose only real restrictions are those you put on yourself - and that is how you must treat it. It means that how much money you make entirely depends on you. You are your own boss. You have total control over your profits by being knowledgeable about investing and real estate, as well as being familiar with foreclosure laws and loan structures, understanding the psychology behind selling and buying, and learning your rules and responsibilities as an owner or seller.

As long as you know what you're really doing, it can almost guarantee you can make money. Unlike a lot of other investments, you are able to depend on one thing with real estate. You are able to eventually make a profit on almost any kind of property you have – on the condition that you paid a practical amount for it in the first place. The value of real estate goes up and down depending on the economy. When real estate prices go down, it's inevitable for them to go back up again.

If you have decided to invest in rental properties, then expect to have a steady flow of income – as long as you're making sure that they are well-maintained. Here's one universal truth about real estate: housing will always be in demand. People will always need it – after all, shelter is at the first level of Maslow's hierarchy of needs. And even in the most challenging markets, rental prices rarely drop much. If you are able to keep your rental units filled with good tenants who pay on time, you can rely on the income from those units to settle mortgage and maintenance expenses to eventually generate profit.

So, the bottom line here is that real estate is a form of investment that takes many years but is a sure way to generate profits. Only if you ignore all the "be a millionaire overnight" promises and false publicity, you will find the real truth: investing in real estate is one of the best ways to be financially stable. And that, after all, is the best reason why you should consider investing in real estate.

1.1 Why It's the Best Vehicle to Reach Financial Freedom

Is it your goal to be rich? Now, you probably think that real estate could be the answer to make this happen. Even though this might be partially true, money isn't necessarily the major benefit of pursuing real estate investment. Personally, I think that the main reward of pushing through this endeavour is to finally live your life just the way you want to. In this sub-chapter, let's dig deeper into how real estate investment can eventually help you reach that form of freedom.

Do you work hard at the moment? Do you think you're not living your life now due to the time and dedication you put in your current work? With the amount of work you're probably dealing with at the moment, do you still have time to spend with your friends and family? I'm pretty sure that you can hardly do that with the time you need to spend at work.

Now, ask yourself… Is it really worth it? Is that really the only way for you to make money?

Fortunately, I realized early in life that working too much during your best years just to reach your goal is not worth it if you're sacrificing the time you could have spent with your family and other people important to you, doing the things that you couldn't do when you're old and ill. If you're starting to feel that life is simply passing you by, then reconsider your decisions, and consider finding a new way to earn a living.

At some point in your life, you may come to the realization that working to afford what you need and want is actually obstructing you from reaching happiness and satisfaction. The stress you get from your workplace, the demands thrown at you by your condescending boss, and juggling all of these with social and family life can be pretty overwhelming to the point that life seems to be pushing you in the pit of misery. This could be quite a push to come to a decision to finally leave the life of a rat race and work toward financial freedom.

Investing in real estate is definitely one of the best ways you can opt for to escape the rat race and earn a living without having to sacrifice other important moments and people of your life. Real estate investment makes a lot of sense when you want to have enough money to support your and your family's needs without stressing too much about working.

With the help of profitable rental properties, you are able to have income even if you decide to quit your current full-time job. But before signing any resignation form, it's extremely important to make yourself knowledgeable about the right steps you need to take in order to build your own portfolio of assets that are going to serve as your source of income.

Money is very important to many people, while there are still some who might argue that happiness is more important. But do you really have to choose just one? Personally, I'd have both of them as much as possible. And yes, it's pretty achievable! So, I urge you to try to live your life how you want it to be, and one of the ways to do that is to invest in real estate.

1.2 Depreciation vs Appreciation

You've probably heard of these terms before aside from real estate; these terms also relate to the value of the currency, stocks, and bonds. However, in the world of real estate, appreciation and depreciation have a little different meaning. Okay, so basically, depreciation is when the value of a property goes down, and appreciation is when the value of a property goes up.

1.2.1 Why Appreciation and Depreciation Happen?

Appreciation may occur when there are changes in the supply and demand of a product or service. When the supply go up and the demand goes down, that's when depreciation comes into the picture.

Here are the most common reasons that lead to depreciation:

- ❖ A massive decline in the market
- ❖ Leaving the property unmaintained
- ❖ Changes in the local neighbourhood

On the other hand, things that can lead to appreciation include:

- ❖ Developments in the nearby areas
- ❖ Home expansion and general improvement
- ❖ Road improvements

The changes in the value of an asset can vary significantly over time. Other assets, which are also known as long-term assets, may lose or gain more value gradually over time.

1.3 Equity Explained

Equity is another term you need to understand when you're getting into real estate investment. Basically, equity is the difference between the property's market value and the money that is owed to the lender. The equity is the money you would get when the mortgage is paid off if you decide to sell the property.

Okay, let me give you a simple example to make it easier for you to understand: Let's say the market value of your property is $300,000 and you owe $200,000 for the mortgage. Your equity then is $100,000 if you happen to sell the property at fair market value.

"Net" Equity

On the other hand, what we call as net equity is different from gross equity. It is your gross equity minus the expenses spent in selling the property. These costs might include the commissions for the realtor, unpaid property taxes, and any closing expenses you have to settle.

Okay, let's give you another example. Let's say the property amounts to $300,000, and it has $200,000 mortgage; then it is going to have $100,000 as equity. But there's a BUT – you owe a commission of $15,000 to your realtor. But keep in mind that you also have to settle the closing expenses like title charges, escrow fees, and tax proration, which may add somewhere around $5,000 in seller-paid expenses. Now, subtract those numbers from your equity.

All in all, net equity is the amount you'd actually keep when the deal is closed.

1.3.1 Building Home Equity

There are many different ways in which homeowners can build home equity. The amount of down payment you put on a property makes the initial mortgage much lower. For instance, if you put in 30% down payment on a property that is valued at $100,000, then you'd start with an equity of $30,000 even before making a mortgage payment. Then the remaining $70,000 would be the mortgage.

Pay Attention to the Mortgage Payment

With every mortgage payment you make, you are building equity. Each payment you make creates a difference in the principal balance that you owe. Every payment also comes with interest on the loan and normally property tax and insurance premium payments too. As you slowly settle mortgage payments and you are able to make extra payments to apply to the principal, your equity goes up.

When Making Home Improvements

Your equity goes up if you make home improvements that upsurge your property's fair market value. For instance, you might have to spend $40,000 to remodel a part of the house, which makes the market value of the property go up by $20,000. Now you have increased your equity by $20,000, assuming you did not take out a home equity loan to afford that new kitchen.

Comparable Sales

Your property's fair market value can go up because the other houses in your area are currently selling for a higher amount. You may have purchased your home a couple of years ago for $150,000 and laid out 20% down payment for it. The same homes are now selling for about $180,000. Your equity in the home has gone up by $30,000 because of this increase.

This rise is also hypothetical. You must sell the home in order to realize this equity. But then again, it's going to be reflected in an appraisal.

1.3.2 How to Reduce Home Equity?

You could also see your home equity go down. Values went down in almost every real estate market in the country in the past few years. When the value of housing falls, equity goes down with it. Your equity goes down if homes sell for less in your area, mainly when you are underwater on your mortgage or on the edge of it.

You might have purchased a home for $300,000 with 20% down payment, which is $60,000. But then, the real estate market went down, and now the same properties are selling for $200,000. Your property value has gone down by $100,000, so you no longer have any equity in the property. If you sold your property for $200,000, you would need to pay out of pocket in order to pay the mortgage lender to settle the difference.

You could also reduce your equity by increasing the principal loans on the property. If you refinance your mortgage or take another mortgage or home equity loan, you will most likely reduce your equity.

If the property burns down or is otherwise ruined in a natural disaster and you happen to not have enough insurance coverage to make up for the loss, then it just means that you have lost your home as well as your equity.

The expenses needed to fix the problems will use up your equity position if you do not consistently make repairs to the home as things decline or stop working properly.

By the end of the deal, you'll find out the equity that comes with the property. If you are able to negotiate a better selling price, you will increase the equity in the deal. And if you happen to not pay for repairs as requested by the purchaser or give the buyer credit for closing expenses, your equity will go up.

1.4 Difference between Assets and Liabilities

Whether you are an accounting expert or not, it's extremely important for you to know the basics of assets and liabilities. Being able to know the difference between the two financial accounts might make all the difference between becoming rich or becoming poor. Now, in this sub-chapter, I want to dig deep into the difference between these two accounts and to offer you some basic knowledge that even laypersons will understand.

1.4.1 Assets Explained

Assets are anything that could be owned by a person or business and that carry a positive cash value. In other words, assets produce income. Here are some examples of assets: real estate, investment, and businesses – all of these can generate income. Assets are things that will give you return on investment.

Now, there are three classes that assets could be categorized under. These are current assets, fixed assets, and intangible assets. By being aware of the difference between these 3 classifications, you can easily understand how to record revenue on financial statements.

Current assets are cash-on-hand or assets that you can turn into cash within a short period of time. Current assets fund daily operations. Companies make use of current assets in order to run their daily operations as this is better than using the money on interest from short-term financing. There are 5 accounts listed under current assets. These accounts include investments, cash, accounts receivable, prepaid expenses and inventory.

Fixed assets are known to be tangible property. Fixed assets cannot be easily turned into cash, unlike current assets. Some of the examples of fixed assets are machines and equipment, property, and buildings. This may also include computers. Fixed assets get special tax treatment and could also be denigrated.

Intangible assets are the items that can't be touched physically. These items could be turned into cash, but they normally hold value to the individual or business that represent it. Some of the examples of intangible assets include trademarks, patents, and copyrights. You will have two different types of intangible assets that are known as the legal intangibles and competitive intangibles. It is recommended that you see your accountant for further advice on intangible assets too.

1.4.2 Liabilities Explained

Now that the assets are clearer to you, let's talk about their evil twin – liabilities. Liabilities are anything that's owned by a person or business that have to be repaid. Unlike assets, liabilities do not generate money, but instead, costs us money. Liabilities are debts that should be repaid back and normally with interest.

There are two categories of liabilities. The first one is the current liabilities, and the other one is long-term liabilities. Both of these classes of liabilities have to be paid back and are counted as debt.

Current liabilities are considered debt that should be paid back within a period of one year. This debt normally is repaid through the current assets account, then again, this is not always the case. There are a lot of different categories of current liabilities. They include accounts payable, notes payable, dividends payable, and short-term debt.

Now that I have explained the differences between assets and liabilities, it has to be stated that it's in the best interest of both the individual and business to have a lot more assets and fewer liabilities. This is how you become wealthy, as you try to not get too many liabilities, particularly if the assets that generate income cannot afford them.

What other people usually invest in and why real estate is the best option for stability because of capital growth.

Where to invest money is a question that has no fixed answer as it changes constantly with time. By investing your money safely, you earn next to nothing. On the other hand, by investing your money in a riskier asset, trouble is almost always inevitable. So, the question is where do people invest and why real estate could be the best way to go.

In more than 20 years of investing money, I have never found the question of *"where to invest your money"* harder than it is now. It is a whole new scenario where interest rates are very low in a weak or ever-changing economy. Now, let's make the best of it and check out the alternatives.

For most investors, the answer to this question begins with mutual funds; it's the investment of choice providing a lot of possibilities. Let's begin at the safest funds being offered.

Money funds place your money in safe money market securities and then pay interest in the form of dividends that go up when interest rates rise and go down when rates decrease. They currently pay returns that are close to zero after expenses, emulating the condition of the current money market. Eventually, interest rates will go up and then money funds might look better.

In the meantime, check out the tax-free versions that pay interest that's free from federal income tax. Whether you believe it or not, a lot of them are paying a higher bonus yield than their taxable counterparts.

Bond funds have been the common answer to where to invest your money in order to earn more interest income. That is good news. On the other hand, the bad news is that, when it comes to investing money and changes in interest rates, they are the opposite of money funds. Bond funds do not get more attractive as interest rates increase. Instead, they lose money, and so do their investors.

1.5 Some of the Most Popular Investment Options Today

Stocks

Stocks are risky and need a lot of research. However, even though this is the case, stocks may offer highly rewarding ROI.

Cryptocurrency

After Bitcoin suddenly overtook the market, people started investing in it, and more cryptocurrencies came out in the market. The problem about this, however, is that the value of it may change rapidly and drastically.

Money Market Funds and Accounts

Money market funds and accounts are popular options because of their extremely low risk. Money market funds invest in low risk and liquid securities like cash equivalent securities, cash, and US Treasury.

Savings Accounts

Savings accounts are also considered very safe and most liquid investment next to cash. They pay very low interest – averagely just a little over 2% as of 2019.

Despite the popularity of different options mentioned above, investing in the real estate market remains one of the best options.

Real estate investment is the purchase of a future income stream from a property and could offer a lot of advantages over other types of investments, which include potentially higher returns, inflation hedging, stability, and variation.

1.5.1 Investing at a Young Age

Investing while you're young is a habit that we, as a society, have to teach the youth. It's not enough that we let the youth find it out themselves. We have to provide the youngsters with formal education not just about the importance of investing at a young age but also about the way they can do it wisely.

What are the benefits of investing at a young age?

First of all, investing at a young age helps you get your much-needed head start, which is very important in maximizing the benefit of letting investments grow over time. If you start to invest early, you get more time in your life to let your investments grow; this is due to the benefits of compound interest and letting your investments increase and grow in value.

Another benefit of investing at an early age is that it gives you more time to recover from any mistakes. If you happen to end up losing some of the money you saved in the market, you'll be able to have more time to recover before actually needing the money if you're planning to invest on a long-term basis.

Furthermore, investing while you're young gives you the flexibility to make riskier investments. In case you lose a great amount of money at a young age, you'll have a lot of time ahead of you to recover from your losses and start again. On the other hand, if you choose to invest while you are a little bit older, then you might be much less risk-averse because you are not able to afford losing money, and you wouldn't have a lot of time on your side to recoup from the losses, before you need to take the money out of the market.

On top of that, you have to keep in mind that investing is a learning process. This means that investing while you're young will give you more time to learn from your mistakes and to set realistic goals that you know you can achieve later in life. Investing at a young age, if done properly, might mean that you'll have a better quality of life as you grow old. By failing to invest properly in your youth, the quality of your life might actually become worse in later years because you'll not have built up your future retirement funds appropriately.

Chapter 2

GETTING STARTED WITH OR WITHOUT MONEY

A lot of people believe that investing in real estate requires a lot of money.

But the truth is, this is still possible with little to no money at all! With many sources of funds available today, real estate investing has become accessible to people of any walk of life.

As opposed to many people's belief, the amount of money you invest will not make or break the deal you are going to do. It is a mistake to stop yourself from diving into the real estate world. Here are different ways you can invest in a real estate business with little to no money.

❖ Borrow the Money

This is possibly the easiest way to buy a property without making a down payment out of your pocket. You can either search for a lender that offers a low-interest rate or make use of a home equity or other type of credit loan that will still provide you with the tax benefits of a normal mortgage. You could also borrow funds from a real estate broker – arrange to borrow the commission of broker for a short period of time and use the funds as the down payment.

❖ **Seller Financing**

Another way to get started with real estate investment without making a down payment is with the help of the seller himself. If ever a seller refuses your down payment, you can ask if you can just pay higher monthly payments instead. There are also cases when the seller would be willing to pay for the down payment just to sell the house faster.

❖ **Rent to Own**

A lot of investors have no idea that they may be able to rent a property from the owner and eventually have the opportunity to purchase it. Depending on the terms of the lease agreement, of course, the buyer and seller can negotiate the total amount to be paid at the time agreed for living in the property. With this agreement, the renter will be able to buy the property at a certain price in a specific timeframe. Normally, the rental payments – might be partial or all – are going to be credited toward the total purchase price of the property.

❖ Use Your Valuable Personal Property

If you own anything valuable, you can use it as a down payment as a substitute for money. Do you have anything that you believe is more valuable than the price of the down payment? Some of the things you can use in replacement to cash are vehicles, jewellery, campers, boats, gadgets, appliances, and furniture.

❖ Shoulder the Seller's Debts

If you find a seller who is in need of cash to pay off other debts, you can offer to shoulder those debts rather than making a down payment.

❖ Find a Partner

This is another way to purchase a property without a down payment – search for other cash buyers. But then again, you have to be very careful with this one as this could be quite messy. So, how this works is you may organize the deal on a smaller scale by bringing in a person or two. In exchange for the financing, you can promise to take the responsibilities of setting up the deal and dealing with the real estate investment. This is something you can also do with the seller himself.

❖ Set Irresistible Offers

There are owners who might be willing to accept a higher price for the property, even though it means you have to pay with instalment, in lieu of accepting a down payment.

❖ Try Wholesaling

Let's say a wholesaler finds a property that is below market value. A wholesaler would acquire that property under contract with the seller and then assign or sell that contract to another buyer or investor, and that investor or buyer would complete the transaction with the seller. The wholesaler is not required to make any improvement on the property at all. The only responsibility is to get it under contract and sell the contract to another investor that's looking for a worn-down house that requires repair.

❖ Combine Mortgages

If you happen to have an existing property, you can combine mortgages in order to pay the seller with cash at closing without making use of your own money. You may also suggest that the seller place a second mortgage on the first and keep the cash, while you, on the other hand, shoulder both loans.

❖ Turn Your House into a Multi-rental

Also known as house hacking, multi-rental is a free way to start up a real estate business. And not only you can make money out of it, but you can also live in it for free! Okay, so the idea behind it is simple… you purchase a multifamily property (2 to 4 units), move into any of these units, and rent out the other units to others. Your tenants will be the ones to cover and pay off the mortgage and other house expenses.

Do your Research

There are specific sellers that might be more willing to accept no money down offers on a property than others. If the property has been available on the market for a long time or is advertised as a must sell, then the seller might be more than willing to agree with your offer. On top of this, just like any other real estate investment, make sure to do research on it beforehand.

2.1 What Are Carrying Costs on a Real Estate Investment

To put it simply, real estate carrying costs are the costs you sustain by reason of your ownership of a specific piece of property. There are properties that are "cash-flow positive," and there are also some that are "cash-flow negative", which means that some properties earn more money in comparison to what they actually cost in order to maintain and some earn less than the "carrying costs". The ones that earn less are normally acquired by the owner for residential or recreational purposes. Some investment properties could be cash-flow negative if one can fairly predict that the resale value of the property will go up to an extent that will recover the negative cash-flow throughout the period of ownership and, presumably some profit as well.

The standard real estate carrying costs include:

- ❖ Homeowners' association (HOA) dues
- ❖ Insurance
- ❖ Maintenance
- ❖ Property taxes
- ❖ Your mortgage payments

However, there are also some investors who consider marketing expenses as holding costs if they are done on a recurring basis. There are different carrying costs for different types of investors: fix and flippers and buy-and-hold investors.

2.1.1 Real Estate Carrying Costs for Fix and Flippers

A fix-and-flip investor buys a property with the plan of renovating it and selling it for a profit. The real estate holding costs are the expenses connected with keeping the property before selling it. These carrying costs always depend on the fix and flipper's budget. They must know how much the carrying costs are going to be, so they know how much it will cost to flip a property.

Fix-and-flip carrying costs normally consist of:

- ❖ Property taxes
- ❖ Property insurance
- ❖ Mortgage payment
- ❖ Utilities
- ❖ HOA fees
- ❖ Marketing fees

Remember that acquisition costs, rehab costs, and real estate agent fees aren't normally considered carrying costs since they are one-time payments and not accrued on a recurring basis.

2.1.2 Real Estate Carrying Costs for Buy-and-Hold Investors

Buy and hold real estate is a long-term investment method. This is where an investor buys a property and keeps or holds onto it for as long as he wants. This investor may have the intention of selling it eventually or rent it out to cover the money spent to own it.

Buy-and-hold investment property carrying costs include:

- ❖ Property taxes
- ❖ Rental property insurance
- ❖ Mortgage payment
- ❖ Utilities
- ❖ Maintenance

- ❖ HOA Fees

- ❖ Property management fees

- ❖ Marketing fees

2.1.3 Examples of Real Estate Carrying Costs

Check out some of the examples of carrying costs and how they affect your ROI.

Let's assume the following costs on a fix-and-flip project:

Acquisition Costs

Down payment: $30,000

Closing costs: $15,000

Mortgage amount: $150,000

Total Acquisition Costs: $195,000

Monthly Carrying Costs

Mortgage payment: $1,000

Property taxes: $300

Property insurance: $100

Utilities: $100

HOA fees: $100

Marketing fees: $150

Total Monthly Carrying Costs: $1,950

Now, let's say that it takes you about 3 months to fix and sell the property; your rehab and other expenses to sell the property are $25,000, and you sell the property for $300,000.

The total investment is the carrying costs multiplied by 3 then add the acquisition costs, rehab, and sales expenses.

$1,950 x 3 = $5,850

$5,850 + $195,000 + $30,000 = $230,850, which then becomes your total investment.

In order to know your ROI, you just have to divide your profit by the investment's total amount then multiply it by 100.

Your total profit is the sales price minus the total amount of your investment

$300,000 – $230,850= $69,150 profit

$69,150/$230,850= 0.30 x 100 = 30 % ROI

The calculation above shows the profit from one deal, which is generally how fix and flippers do calculation of their ROI on a per property basis.

Based on this example, you can calculate the total monthly carrying costs to help you calculate the budget you need to get into the real estate investment business. They also heavily influence your ROI. The shorter your timeline is and the lower your carrying costs are, the higher your ROI will be, all other things being equal.

2.2 Tips on Dealing with Real Estate Carrying Costs

Dealing and managing the carrying cost is one of the top responsibilities of a real estate investor. This is very important because by overlooking this, you can potentially go over the specified budget. This can cause a decrease in ROI.

But then again, if you are well aware of your carrying costs upfront, you are able to account for them, plan consequently, and don't get out of your budget. Here are important things you have to do to control the real estate carrying costs:

❖ Be Aware of the Real Estate Holding Expenses Upfront

As an investor, you have to understand your real estate carrying costs right before signing any contract. By doing this, you will know if you can afford the property, what are the total costs to own the property, and how much the rent should be.

❖ Keep Your Eyes on the Rehab Supplies

Rehab supplies influence the total carrying costs. Vacant property has higher theft compared to an occupied one. The occurrences of theft could increase the carrying costs and at the same time, lower the ROI.

❖ Add the Renovation Expenses to the Total Expenses

Renovations affect the real estate holding expenses by a great deal. Most of the time, investors overlook the additional financing and utility expenses once the renovations run over the specified timeline.

2.3 Top Options to Finance Your Investment with Limited Funds

While these methods were mentioned in our previous list, let's go deeper into these two options as I think these are two of the options I would always recommend.

2.3.1 Lease Option Agreement

This home buying option can be used when buyers are engaged in credit repair but are not able to qualify for bank financing. Basically, lease options are a layaway plan that lets the buyers settle the payment through monthly instalments for a prearranged amount of time.

A lease-purchase option agreement could be planned to meet the needs of both parties but should stand by state laws. Most sellers need a down payment in order to secure the property for sale and pay a portion of monthly rental payments toward the purchase of the property.

Lease option contracts should be prepared by an estate lawyer. This form of contract applies different rules depending on the state and might involve a lease option to buy, purchase agreement, or lease option.

Types of Lease Purchase Option Agreements

Lease options are the most commonly used contract for rent-to-own properties. Buyers need to offer 'options' money in order to secure the home that is being purchased. The main setback of using option money, however, is that funds are non-refundable and don't apply toward the purchase price.

Sellers are not allowed to list the property for sale when lease options are used. Furthermore, lease options contracts couldn't be sold or assigned without being approved by both parties. If a tenant defaults on their contract or cannot acquire bank financing when the contract expires, they forfeit all the funds used toward the purchase.

Lease purchase agreements are the second type and are the most complicated lease-to-own contract. Buyers are legally allowed to buy real estate once the contract expires. If they happen to default on the purchase contract, they might have to deal with legal consequences. So, it's important to know all the risks involved before they enter into a lease-purchase option agreement.

Buyers must perform due diligence by acquiring real estate assessments as well as home inspections. Buyers must get comparable sales reports in order to figure out the fair market value. Sellers are able to choose to lock-in the purchase price when lease-purchase agreements are drafted or ask buyers to pay fair market value once the contract expires.

Buyers are able to offer a lump sum down payment or pay it in instalments. For instance, the seller requires a $30,000 down payment but lets the buyer pay $20% of it upfront and extend the remaining throughout the term of the agreement.

A part of the rent money is put toward the purchase value. Sellers hardly assign 100 per cent of rent money, but this happens in some cases. Averagely, sellers save 10% to 40% of the monthly rent.

Buyers that have poor credit score should participate in credit repair strategies in order to boost their credit scores and get rid of the bad credit in order for them to qualify for a home mortgage loan once the effect of the lease option finishes.

Steps to Acquiring Lease Option Agreement

Selling real estate on lease option agreement is a great technique allowing you to tap into a big sea of people that are interested in buying a property but for some reason, are not quite able to make the purchase at the moment. If you're one of these people, here are the steps to follow to get into this agreement.

Step 1: Find the Property to Buy

Search for properties in your neighbourhood or in a desirable location somewhere else. Homeowners sometimes advertise their houses as lease-to-own. You may want to drive around and search for signs. Usually, the sign will tell the purchase price as well as the monthly rent. Also, search online sites for these sort of properties as well.

Step 2: Research the Home and the Owner

Check the reason why the homeowner is selling it. Make sure that the seller is a motivated seller and want to get rid of the property quickly because of maybe wanting a bigger house, or the property has negative equity, or they're moving to a new place for work, etc. Watch out for the signs the owner is facing financial trouble. Remember that if the owner goes bankrupt while you are leasing it, they will probably lose the house and you will also be evicted at the same time. Because of this, you have to make sure that the seller is financially stable.

Step 3: Analyse Tax Records

You are able to acquire property tax records from the tax assessor's office. See to it that the person you have been working with is really the owner. There are times when the person who faces you is a fraudster and just pretending to be the owner.

Step 4: Get an appraisal

It's important to know how much the house is worth, in case you end up buying it at the end of the lease. Get a referral to an appraiser from the real estate agent. You can also search the directory of the American Society of Appraisers.

Step 5: Have the Home Inspected

See if there are any defects in the home now – whether they are major or minor. It's not nice to start staying there and then realize that the house has a serious structural defect. You can get a real estate agent to do the inspection, which may cost you between $300 and $600.

Step 6: Review the title report

A title report is going to tell you how long the seller has the house to his name. Preferably, the seller owned the property for years already. Someone who has owned the property for a long time must have equity built up in the home and are possibly more stable.

Step 7: See if You Will Qualify for a Mortgage

You do not need a mortgage while you're renting. But you will need it later if you choose to purchase the house at the end of the lease period. Just make sure your credit is not so bad by this time, or you won't get qualified.

Step 8: Negotiate the Purchase Price

Negotiate the price you want to pay if you want to buy the property at the end of the lease. Remember it's an option to buy not an obligation, and the contract you set up for this should state this.

Step 9: Close the Deal

Closing the deal can be a lengthy process. The lender may want an appraisal, inspection, and of course, the title report. You will need to review any disclosures from the seller regarding the defects in the property. If everything goes well, you must close about 45 days after you exercise the option.

2.3.2 Real Estate Wholesaling

Another option you can use when investing in real estate business with limited funds is wholesaling. This is one of the methods you can use to generate money without ever owning property or putting up a huge amount of money for the home. You are able to tie up the property by putting it under contract for a minimal fee, and then you sell it for a higher price compared to the price that was accepted when you put it under the agreement.

Wholesaling is a short-term investing method. Many people think that it's the same as fixing and flipping, but the two have significant differences. Wholesaling real estate is the way to go for those who don't have a lot of money on the table; the downside of this, however, is the confusion it can cause as well as the complicated legality and contracts. When becoming a wholesaler, always stay compliant to the rules and regulations to avoid getting into any lawsuits etc.

Steps to Real Estate Wholesaling

Step 1: Search for a Property to Wholesale

The best type of properties to wholesale are the distressed ones. This is because you can buy them under market value. Distressed properties are the ones in critical condition or the ones that the owners want to get rid of as soon as possible. Choosing this type of property will let you sell the property at a higher price, giving you a big return on investment.

Step 2: Set an Offer that will Convince the Owner to Sell It

The moment you have identified a property with a good deal, the next step is to convince the property owner to sell it to you. This is a very important step since it is going to help you secure the properties to wholesale and generate a profit.

When you're approaching the homeowner, it's important to carry it out it in a delicate way. Because a wholesaler isn't a traditional real estate expert, they'll have to gain the trust of the homeowner before going through. This could be done by being polite, professional, and punctual when meeting the homeowner.

Step 3: Sign the Contract

The homeowner will have to approve and sign the contract. You can create your own contract, but if you want it to look more professional, you can hire a local agent or attorney to set up the contract for you. The latter is the better option so you can make sure that the contract follows the Agreement of Sale.

Step 4: Search for the Right People in the Team

There are three important team members you need to have to run this project better. These are a contractor, title company, and an appraiser. With these people on your team, you can assure that you can maintain the company's level of professionalism and that you can run your business according to how it should be. Having these people in your team will help you save time and money in due course.

Step 5: Evaluate the Needs of the Property for Renovation

By evaluating what renovations are needed in the property, you will know the expenses and make sure they will work according to your plan to make money off the deal. A property that requires renovations can potentially earn you more money. This margin will also help you generate money. That's why it's important that you know how much renovation the property needs as this gives you an idea of how much return you'll get from it.

Step 6: Find a Buyer

You now found a property to wholesale, hired the right professionals to help you, and are aware of what repairs the property needs. Finding the buyer will be the next step. You're not looking for a family or a first-time buyer, but rather, it is going to be an investor or a contractor who wants to buy the property to repair it.

You have to find a buyer immediately because there is going to be a settlement date on the contract that you have to follow. When the potential buyers start calling you about the property, save their info, even if it turns out that your property is not what they are looking for.

Step 7: Negotiate a Deal with the Buyer

When you've finally found the buyer that is interested in buying the property, negotiating the deal would be the next step. It's important to negotiate as it is going to help you determine how much money you will make from this deal. The difference between how much you bought the property for and what you are wholesaling it for will be the total amount of profit you make.

While you're negotiating with the buyer, use the estimate of the contractor to your advantage. Tell the potential buyer that you have other buyers that are interested in the property, so if they want to buy it, they must act fast. The buyer must leave a deposit, which can be held in escrow until things get settled.

Step 8: Closing on the Wholesale Property

Now to the final step... The closing, also known as the settlement, has to be made at the title company's office and is going to last about one and a half-hour. Both parties are going to be there as the deed is being transferred to its new owner. When it's done, it is going to be the completion of the wholesale deal.

Chapter 3

How to Find Lucrative Properties

All good investors are aware of the importance of knowing how to find and choose properties that are going to be profitable. So, whether you're a seasoned investor or simply starting out, finding where to find a property is something many real estate investors may find challenging. Here are different effective ways you can follow:

I. Search for a Beginner Property with Good Potential

You don't have to go too far to find the best property. The first place to look at is your own town, your own area. You are familiar with it, so you'll know which areas are good and which are the ones that are bad. You are far less likely to lose money when you are familiar with your way around. Starting small is the best way to be a real estate shark. In this industry, going big is likely to lead to going home.

Set a Clear Goal

Setting a clear goal shouldn't be too difficult. Figure out as early as possible how much money you are willing to invest and how much of a return you are trying to reach by the end of the year. For example, your goal could be to get at least 50% of what you spent by the end of the year from the time the business starts spending money. Your goal can surely help you determine the type of property suitable for you.

Make Sure that Everything You Are Dealing with is Legal

This might be surprising, but a lot of property owners rent out their units in places they are not allowed to legally. So, you have to make sure that the rental is legal by confirming it at the registrar's office.

Buy the Neighbourhood, Not the House

A house of the same size and quality only a couple of blocks away can be worth 20% more. All towns have a good and bad neighbourhood, and you want to choose a good neighbourhood that your budget can afford.

Don't Settle for the First One You see

It's so easy to fall in love with the first property we see, but try to hold back because you might find better ones! It's best to look at all the options available and then shortlist all the ones you like until you find the one you think is best for you.

Get Help from a Local Broker

You can check all the news ads and all the websites that state the available properties in your area, but no one knows better than a local broker. If you do great research, they surely can do it better!

II. Know What to Check Out

Before putting in money into any property for sale, make sure you know the history of it. Based on that, you can make predictions on how it is going to turn out after you buy it.

Don't Think the Taxes Will Stay the Same

Taxes change annually and could go up drastically after buying it.

Know the Factors in the Cost of Your Tenants Moving in and Out

The huge surprise for most new landlords is the costs of tenant turnover, such as advertising for a new tenant, cleaning fees, agent fees, repainting, and adding new basic furniture.

Get an Insurance Quote Beforehand

You have to keep in mind that insurance on an investment property is much more expensive compared to the house insurance.

Find Out the Realistic Maintenance Expenses

If the property is made of brick, then you probably wouldn't have to paint, and you don't have to spend on maintaining the condition of the wood. Of course, it is a lot easier to maintain a smaller property compared to a bigger one. On top of that, more units mean more money being spent. When you buy a property that is located miles away, then it means you'd have to spend more money on gas to drive around.

III. Get Yourself a Good Partner

Searching for a good business partner is as tough as finding a good property. The best real estate partners you can have are the ones who carry the traits and skills you don't have. If you are good with negotiation but don't know much about finance, then find one that is good with it. Or if you are good with marketing but find managing clients overwhelming, find the one that's an expert in it. A lot of today's best real estate partnerships are a combination of someone with a lot of money and someone who has the knowledge to run it.

Chapter 4

HOW TO SPOT A GOOD DEAL

Whether you're planning to flip a house, buying a property to eventually turn it into rental space, or do something completely different to it, one thing is for sure: it has to be a great deal. Let me give you some simple tips that will guide you in finding the better deals in real estate investment regardless of what your plans are.

1. Consider purchasing a bank-foreclosed property

When someone was not able to pay a mortgage, and it has been a long period of time, the lender will eventually repossess the property and kick out the occupants. When the home is empty, the lender will then list the house for sale on the market, with the help of a local real estate agent to list it.

2. Be the first to make the offer

In the world of real estate, you have to keep in mind that the higher offer is not the only one that always wins, but the one that offers first. So, if you're seeking a great deal, make sure to be the faster one! Get pre-approved by a bank right away, jump off the property you think is best for your intentions. Ask the real estate agents you know to inform you about the latest offerings available in the market in case you find them interesting. And don't waste your time and check it out right away and send off an offer.

3. Connect with absentee owners in private

Due to the high demand of the real estate market, it becomes more challenging to find great deals in real estate. In several areas, a single house listed on the market might receive a dozen or more offers within its first few days.

And with this situation, one of the best kinds of sellers to find is absentee owners, which simply means a person who owns a property but does not live there anymore. These people could be landlords or owners who inherited the property and are just uncertain about what to do with them.

There are many different ways you can find them, and here are those ways:

- ❖ Drive around and search for houses that may look vacant

- ❖ Buy a public record list from an aggregate-list site like ListSource.com

- ❖ Search on craigslist or even post an ad on it saying you're searching for abandoned properties

4. Know what good deals really are

Last, but not least, you have to learn how to determine whether the deal is good or bad! Don't settle for the first thing you find as you'll almost always find more options. Remember that a "good deal" doesn't always mean the cheaper one. You have to look at everything that comes with the deal, like where is it located, how much renovation is needed, or how clean the title is.

Whether you're planning to purchase an investment property, purchase a home to give a roof to your family, or purchase a property for other reasons, always keep in mind that in order to make money, you need to spend money. Remember that finding a good deal is key to having quick equity.

4.1 What to Look for When Looking for Real Estate

Continuous income, stability, appreciation, tax benefits, great returns – the arguments for investing in long-term, hold-to-rent real estate definitely make a lot of sense. And while buying a property is always exciting, it can also be pretty scary, stressful, and more than a bit painful as you make your way through approvals, paperwork, and "hoops" of different shapes and sizes.

In order to help you navigate the process a bit easier, here are important things to look for when looking for real estate.

- **A Great Location**

"Location, location, location…" It is pretty obvious why people put so much importance on the location of the real estate. First of all, a good location is the key to getting a good ROI. It also determines the amount of rent you earn, the quality of your renter, and the vacancy rate you may experience.

A neighbourhood that gives you access to many amenities would be your best bet when you are planning to hold-and-rent. Great schools, a big job market, public transportation, recreation area, shopping centres, restaurants, post offices, libraries, medical centres, and entertainment places are some of the things that are going to make your rental appealing to your prospective tenants.

- **Practical Amenities**

If you are new to the real estate industry, you find it tempting to choose your investment property based on your emotions. That is a common trap, and it is something you don't want to fall into. Keep in mind that you are not going to be living in this rental yourself, so it wouldn't make sense to prioritize your taste and preferences. You might want a unit with a bigger kitchen, but are you sure that it's something that every tenant would want? What if your first tenant would be a busy bachelor who would rather order meals? Do you think the money you paid for having a bigger kitchen is going to be worth it? As long as the amenities are complete, it is enough. This is not to say that you must avoid units with more space – that's still going to be a big bonus, but that shouldn't be a priority.

- **Low Maintenance**

There are investment properties that would take more time to maintain than others. Some of these are student rentals and vacation rentals. Properties in low-quality areas that are not in good shape also have higher turnover rates and will need more work on your part.

Most of the time, the most low-maintenance properties attract stable, long-term tenants. These possibly wouldn't be the flashiest investments on the market, but it's okay. It's always better to opt for something strong and steady, rather than be a flash in the pan.

• The Potential to Appreciate

A good investment is a rental property that brings a lot of value. As an investor, you must appraise the property on two levels: the first is to value it when you buy it and the second is to value it when you're selling it.

When you're buying it, look deep into its potential and envision how you can turn it into something that will generate income. How much more can you charge on it after laying new layers of paint on the walls? What about when you replace the curtains with new ones? By appreciating it even before you bought it, it is going to be easier for you to appreciate it when it's ready for selling.

• Normal, Through and Through

Long-term, hold-to-rent properties could be a great and stable investment – as long as you are smart. Otherwise, you may find yourself in a high-risk situation quickly. When it comes to long-term rentals, "smart" means "normal." It's not your goal to be the next HGTV star. What you want is to have a steady, low-risk investment.

What "normal" means is that you need to look for something more practical, in good, presentable shape – a place people would want to live in. A good example of something practical is a 3-bedroom, 2-bath house with a good layout for a family, located near major employment centres, shopping market, and school. On the other hand, what is considered impractical is buying a gorgeous updated Victorian property that has a big backyard located in the middle of nowhere.

In finding the right real estate investment, there is one mantra you need to follow: Stick to the basics. While they might not look very enticing at first glance, they could actually be something extremely exciting only if you look at them deeper.

4.2 The Importance of Not Letting Emotions Affect You When Buying Properties

According to real estate agents, emotional mistakes are very common among home investors, who pay too much for their "dream homes" because they put too much of their emotions when buying a property.

However, there's no point for buyers to beat themselves up for getting emotional throughout this process. Buying a property or a house is usually the biggest purchase a person will ever make. So, often, homebuyers need a person or two to stand by their side and remind them how they shouldn't let their emotions decide their investment.

Logic and emotions are two natural traits that clash when combined together when one is shopping. And being able to know how both traits can affect the process of your decisions while shopping for a property can ease stress away and let you feel in control of the buying process.

Now let's take a look at how emotions affect the buying process and how it shouldn't be tolerated. Buyers have to be aware of emotional mistakes a lot of their fellow investors make.

4.2.1 Common emotions that prompt us to make the purchase

Generally, there are three emotional factors that trigger people in making the wrong decisions. Those include the following:

Pain: It becomes the motivating factor why we search for a home in the first place. It might be that a new member of the family is coming, one has to relocate for work, or a person needs a new source of income.

Promise: This motivating factor carries new hope and joy in the future, like having wealth from a continuous source of income from the rental business.

Fear: This emotion makes the person worried that he might be spending a handsome amount of money on something that is not worth it.

A quick emotional attachment

When a potential investor walks into the house, chances are he might fall in love with it right away. They start imagining themselves living it in, changing something in the house to make it the way they want. They start to look way ahead into the future, imagining themselves years after buying it. The tour can easily trigger future hopes and thoughts. On the other hand, if you can't feel these emotions, then it's probably because there's no instant emotional attachment.

Romanticized notions

Most of the time, buyers love to hear the history of the property, particularly about the previous owners, what they do, where they are now, and why did they move. This makes them feel and imagine themselves being in those people's shoes.

Cultural beliefs

Some people base their decisions on certain beliefs or superstitions. For example, in China and Japan, number

9 is believed to be an unlucky number. On top of this, many traditional Chinese families strictly follow Feng Shui.

Influence of colours

Colours can trigger feelings and emotions in people. And that even means paying more money for a house to be painted in specific colours. For example, recent data support the idea that houses that have bathrooms with light pale blue to soft periwinkle blue bathrooms sold for more than the ones with other colours. It's normal for people to want to feel peaceful when they are in their own homes. Furthermore, statistics show that wall interiors painted with neutrals colours such as blue and grey have a better appeal and might indicate that the house was well-taken care of by its old owners.

On the other hand, properties that are painted with darker colours like terracotta sold for way less than the expected price.

There's no denying the fact that emotions can make potential home buyers make bad decisions in investment. This happens more often than you imagine. Some people just pay more than what the properties actually cost.

When homebuyers let their emotions go crazy, it surpasses the logic entirely. But remember that at the end of the day, emotions will always play a part in buying a property; you just have to learn how to limit and control them.

Why We Shouldn't Let Emotions Rule Us

One of the biggest challenges in the sale of a property is the emotional reactions of both parties. It does not matter if you're the buyer, seller, or even the realtor. If either party allows emotions to run the day, things may go differently from how you originally planned them, and it may get ugly.

For the one who is selling the property, emotions root from the fact that they have lived in the home for some time. They built priceless memories in their property –

that is where they raised their kids, built their dreams, and that has been their safe, comfortable place for years. In other words, sellers don't see the property as just a piece of land with a house on it. They see it as something that makes them who they are, which they have to let go and move on from. This personal attachment causes tangled feelings when a buyer offers any bad comments about the property.

For buyers, on the other hand, emotions result from the conscious or subconscious nervousness about having to pay a big amount of money. Whether you admit it or not, it is pretty scary to commit to paying to something that costs more than what you already have in the bank. Of course, this emotion may come as a red flag. For example, you feel like the seller is pushing you too much into buying the property, your feelings might tell you that there might be something wrong with the property that's why the seller is trying to sell it fast.

So, whether you are planning to buy or sell a property, make sure that you can let go or at least control your emotions. Remember that this is a business transaction, and in business, logic comes first.

4.2.2 Which Properties Are the Best to Buy for Rentals?

One of the biggest decisions investors make when looking for property for rentals is to choose which property is the best for this purpose. After all, you will have many options. That's why choosing the one that you must buy should be well-thought-out, and there should be no room for rushed decisions.

But in this chapter, we will talk about the two most common options when it comes to rental properties: condo and a single-family home. Which one is the better option to invest? Let's explore their features, pros and cons, and other factors that will help you decide.

Which one is better? Condo vs Single Family Home

Before getting to the conclusion as to whether condos or single-family home would be a better option for real estate investment, let's look at each type of property first.

❖ Condos

This is a type of rental property that is a multi-family housing unit and is also known as a condominium. This kind of property can be either built as an apartment building or similar to a single-family house.

Usually, the condos are set up as separate units in a bigger residential real estate building. The major difference between apartments, however, lays in the ownership of this type of investment properties. While apartments are usually owned by one person or company, the units in the condos are sold individually.

Another thing is that condos are built as detached houses. And while this is the case, they're considered a different type of investment property compared to single-family homes. That is because even when condos are built as detached homes, they share common facilities like pools, gym, etc.

❖ Single Family Homes

Single-family homes are single detached houses. These types of properties are entirely detached from any other real estate properties. Single-family homes usually have a private yard and direct access to the street. Furthermore, these residential properties don't share any common areas, and community maintenance is not necessary.

The previous characteristics of every property type are just a little part of the subject of condo vs single-family home. In order to have the full picture of the matter, it would be necessary to be familiar with the pros and cons of both rental property types. By knowing these, deciding as to whether you should buy a condo or a single-family home would be much easier.

Advantages and Disadvantages of Buying a Condo

❖ Affordable Real Estate

One of the top reasons as to why condos are considered one of the best real estate investment option is the fact that they are affordable. These income properties are fairly affordable on the standard of the real estate market, especially in comparison to single-family properties. Even beginner low-budget real estate investors can get started by investing in condos and developing their rental property business even more.

❖ Rental Property Management and Maintenance

The management and maintenance are one of the top reasons why investing in a condo is a very popular option. Because the property shares common areas together with other units, an investor isn't required to maintain all of these areas. The job is usually done by community service providers. So, the landlord must spend time and money in the condo unit itself and pay extra fees for the maintenance of common areas. This is not the case with single-family homes.

❖ Higher Demand in the Rental Market

Last but not least, condos have higher demand, therefore finding tenants for them is easier. That means that they bring high occupancy rates and steady rental income. This phenomenon is not rocket science – this is just due to the fact that today's young generation prefers renting multifamily units. Millennials start to think about starting a family and renting a bigger home only later in life. The high demand leads to a high ROI for condominiums.

Of course, just as with everything else, choosing a condo for rental also comes with some disadvantages.

❖ **Rental Restrictions**

First of all, condos usually come with rental restrictions, which might be imposed by the on-site community, for example. A lot of people don't want tenants on the premises of the multifamily homes because tenants might create noise and do damage to the common areas, etc. So, you have to carefully consult with the other owners or the HOA before starting to rent out your new property.

❖ Real Estate Investment Loans

Another problem you might encounter is when you are using real estate investment loans. While condos are normally affordable, financing them is not easy. In fact, you might find it difficult to get traditional mortgage lenders to give you the money for you to use in these properties. There are mortgage lenders that require a high down payment, while some even request the owner to live in the property for a certain period of time before they are allowed to buy it.

4.2.3 Advantages and Disadvantages of Investing in Single Family Home Rentals

❖ Higher Real Estate Appreciation

The biggest advantage of investing in a single-family home is real estate appreciation. By running this type of property as your rental business, you're going to be in full control of maintaining and upgrading the rental property. Through this, you can always increase the resale value of this investment. For this reason alone, a lot of property investors believe that single-family homes are the better rental investment.

❖ Type of Tenant

As mentioned earlier, multifamily units are typically rented by younger people. Sometimes, it is the case that such tenants misbehave and damage the property in some sort of way. When it comes to single-family homes, on the other hand, the tenants are usually young families who would like to settle down. This might give a real estate investor confidence that the rental property is going to be taken good care of.

❖ The Freedom Single-Family Rentals Give

Of course, the freedom that comes with this type of investment is a big advantage. You can rent out the property to whoever you want. You can manage and keep the rental property however you want.

But then again, there are also a few disadvantages that come with investing in single-family homes. Here are some of them.

❖ **Vacancies**

Because condos are more in demand, it might not be as easy for you to find tenants for your property. So, this just means that once the unit goes vacant, there's a high chance for the property to stay like this for a while. Investing in a few multifamily units leads to lower vacancy rates. Since purchasing multiple single-family homes is a bit more complicated, it's not always easy to avoid negative cash flow from time to time.

❖ **Cost**

Last of all is the cost of such an investment. Single-family homes are difficult to finance at first because of their initial property value. Furthermore, the maintenance and renovation of the property are also more expensive compared to condos.

Conclusion

Both condos and single-family homes would be great investment opportunities for investors looking for rental properties. Just make sure that you are aware of the pros and cons, and from there, you can decide which one works best for you.

4.2.4 What below market value means?

Below the market can refer to any kind of investment or purchase that is made at a below the market price. In the world of investment trading, a below the market order is an order to purchase or sell a security at a price that is lower compared to the current market price. In wider terms, below the market may also refer to the price or rate that's lower compared to the current prevailing conditions in an open market. Services or goods that are offered at a lower price compared to the "going," or typical, rate could be considered as below the market.

Purchases made under below the market conditions are good to the buyer since they can obtain goods, investments, or services at a price that's lower than the going rate. Below the market is a common term that could be used by investors as well as investment traders.

Below the Market Trade Orders

Traders and investors might have several platforms available when looking to execute a trade. Institutional investors could usually access different public and non-public trading centres. Retail investors are usually going to execute their trades through a discount brokerage platform or ask their broker to place a trade. In most situations, all investors have the choice to choose the maximum price they want to pay for something.

In a below the market order, an investor who would like to try to meet a better price or position can enter an order to purchase securities at a price that's below the market. In general, trading platforms will lay down the order with a selected price as a limit order.

In a limit order, the investor offers a maximum price they're willing to pay to buy a security. Putting a below the market limit order is going to give a much higher risk of being unsettled in the open market. If the day's price on the specified security never goes below its current trading price or in case it goes up, the limit order wouldn't be placed, and the investor wouldn't take ownership in the security. If the limit order to purchase is filled, the order is going to be placed at the specific price. There are trades in which only a part of the shares might be bought if the broker can't identify sellers for a full lot of requested shares.

Limit orders that let investors identify below the market price for purchasing security will vary from standard market orders. Standard market orders are usually a defaulted order type of trading platform.

Capital gains

Capital gain is a rise in the value of a capital asset real estate or investment, which gives it a higher worth compared to the purchase price. You wouldn't realize the gains until the asset is sold. A capital gain might be considered short-term or long-term and have to be claimed on income taxes.

Understanding Capital Gains

While capital gains are usually associated with funds and stocks because of their inherent price volatility, a capital gain may take place on any security that's sold for a price higher than the purchase price that was paid for it. Realized capital losses and gains happen when an asset is sold, which leads to a taxable event. Sometimes, unrealized gains and losses are referred to as paper gains and losses, which reflect growth or decline in value of the investment that hasn't yet triggered a taxable event.

A capital loss is sustained when there's a decrease in the capital asset value compared to the purchase price of the asset.

4.2.5 Tax Consequences of Capital Gains and Losses

Tax-conscious mutual fund investors have to determine a mutual fund's unrealized gathered capital gains, which are considered as a percentage of its net assets before you invest in a fund with a significant unrealized capital gain factor. This circumstance is referred to as a capital gains exposure to the fund. When distributed by a fund, capital gains are a taxable obligation for the investors of the fund.

Short-term capital gains happen on securities held for a year or less. These gains are taxed as ordinary income derived from the person's tax filing status and attuned gross income. Long-term capital gains are normally taxed at a lower rate compared to regular income. 20% is the long-term capital gains rate in the highest tax bracket. However, 15% is the most common qualifying number for tax-payers.

Capital Gains Distribution by Mutual Funds

Mutual funds that have amassed realized capital gains through the year should distribute those gains to the shareholders. A lot of mutual funds distribute capital gains at the end of the year.

People who are receiving the distribution acquire a 1099-DIV form, which explains the amount of the capital gain distribution and how much is considered short-term and long-term. Once the mutual fund makes a capital gain or bonus distribution, the net asset value (NAV) goes down by the amount of the distribution. A capital gains distribution doesn't affect the total return of the fund.

4.2.6 Understanding ROI in real estate (return on investment)

One important factor that many savvy real estate investors look at when choosing which properties might be profitable for them is the rate of return on rental property.

Return on investment or ROI is an accounting term that defines the percentage of invested money that is earned after the deduction of associated expenses. This is something that could be confusing for a layperson to understand. However, the formula is as simple as this:

$$ROI = \frac{Gain - Cost}{Cost}$$

where:

$Gain = $ Investment gain

$Cost = $ Investment cost

But while the equation seems easy enough to calculate, with real estate, several variables, which include repair and maintenance expenses and means of figuring leverage, come into play, which could affect ROI numbers. In a lot of cases, the ROI is going to be higher if the cost of the investment is lower.

When buying a property, the terms of financing could significantly affect the price of the investment. But then again, using resources such as a mortgage calculator could help you save money on the investment expenses by helping you find favourable interest rates.

Calculating ROI on real estate could be simple or complicated, depending on all the variables involved. In a healthy economy, investing in real estate, may it be residential and commercial, has proven to be extremely profitable. Even during a recessionary economy, when prices go down and cash is scarce, a lot of bargains in real estate are available for investors with the money to invest. When the economy gets back on its feet, as it invariably does, a lot of investors will reap a striking profit.

Chapter 5

SALES & NEGOTIATION TECHNIQUES

If you really want to get into the game and earn real money in the world of real estate investment, then you should master the art of negotiation. What many people don't actually understand about real estate is that it's a business, and therefore whether you are a real estate investor, businessman, lawyer, or even a housewife, negotiations are an important part of life and are most certainly key to attaining success. Ask any successful individuals, and you will see that, for the most part, they've become skilled at negotiation and can normally work things in their odds.

Not everyone knows how negotiation works, but this skill could be learned by anyone as long as they are eager to learn. Along with the drive to succeed and an enthusiasm for learning, anyone who wants to expand his horizons is able to open his doors to very prolific real estate negotiations and deals that can change his life for the better. After all, not everyone is easy to deal with; that's why the art of negotiating is always going to come in handy as a person walks through the journey of life.

Mastering the art of negotiation is usually more complicated than it seems. Good negotiation is one in which both parties could actually gain something valuable. When a party loses while the other one wins, then the wrong negotiating strategies must have been used. Good deals must always benefit both parties, as there might come the point in time when the person you are dealing with can significantly help you in the future.

Let's take this case, for example. A real estate investor wants to sell a property to a buyer who's searching for a house to live in. This investor might want to sell the house at a very high price while the buyer is looking for quality and value for money. This is a give and take scenario and will make both parties win in the situation. The real estate investor can get a high price for the property if the house he is selling is in great shape and the condition preferred by the buyer. The investor earns from the deal while the buyer gets the house that he wants.

While negotiations are a lot more evident in real estate and business deals, this is something we do unconsciously every day. We do it when asking for more time at work. We do it when inviting someone at a party. It is an important skill that people must learn. When done properly, negotiating could be turned into profits and a very comfortable life.

There are people who learn how to negotiate well when they are exposed to individuals from all walks of life. A job that lets someone meet a lot of people significantly helps in improving one's negotiating skills. This, together with reading good books and going to related seminars or classes, helps in developing negotiation skills.

Even if you're trying to avoid them, negotiations are the key to getting what you want and offering a great future for your family. When you learn the art of negotiating, it's going to be a skill that you will always have with you for the rest of your life. It most definitely provides you with a better advantage in any situation you are in.

5.1 How to Negotiate During a Real Estate Transaction

The goal is to have an agreement on the terms of the deal, which include price, timelines, eventualities, and items that might carry with the property. Remember that there will be continuous negotiation until the deal is closed. Here are some scenarios buyers and sellers should prepare for.

Price

Both sellers and buyers would try to negotiate the best price possible for their benefits, and there are many possible reasons for this. Of course, the seller wants to sell the property as expensive as possible while the buyer, on the other hand, would want to pay the lowest amount possible. They usually meet somewhere in between. Buyers don't want to pay more than what the property usually costs, while the seller, on the other hand, wants to make sure that he's getting the right amount of money from the property he is selling.

Closing costs

The prepaid closing expenses for their mortgage have to be paid by the buyer. This is the money that the mortgage lender has in escrow for things such as taxes and insurance. It's acceptable for the buyer to ask a seller to pay for the entire closing costs or up to how much the lender is allowed to pay a contribution. This could be up to 3% of what's included in the mortgage. If a buyer asks the seller to make a franchise on his behalf, they are likely going to need to pay a higher asking price.

Closing date

Sellers are allowed to negotiate for speed when they have to get their capital out of the home quickly, and closing dates are going to affect buyers' monthly cash flow when they own the home. Remember that when a buyer closes on the property, he skips the payment for a mortgage for the following month. They probably want to close at the starting part of the month so that they skip the following month.

Financing contingencies

Many transactions end up being cash; that's why sellers do not tie up their property for 1 to 2 months, which is what is needed when there is a financing contingency in place. Buyers that are trying to compete with all-cash offers have to know if they are capable of dropping the financing eventuality that will make the closing timeline shorter. This is possible for the buyer if they get their mortgage entirely approved before making an offer.

Home warranty

When it comes to the home warranty, the seller can ask or even demand this or the seller can voluntarily offer this. This is a protection plan that covers the appliances and systems of the home, like hot water heater and A/C in the event these things break or require repair or maintenance.

Leaseback

There's no denying the fact that moving to a new place is a process that is highly stressful. If a seller requires a bit of extra time to get into their new home, buyers can offer a zero-cost rent-back for 1 to 3 months to convince the seller to accept the offer over others. Giving the buyer peace of mind is a very effective negotiating tactic.

Home repairs

When the house requires a lot of repairs, this is going to be an opportunity for the buyer to negotiate a lower price. When a home is outdated with appliances that no longer work, cracked walls, or popped ceilings, a buyer could ask for a lower price due to the cost of repairs needed to be done. If the seller doesn't want to make any repairs on the property, then it should be advertised "as is".

Appraisal contingency

If the buyer is getting a mortgage, waiving the appraisal contingency is possible for the buyer to do. But this is only when they make good on the amount of cash to close if for some reason the appraisal falls short, and the bank will lend them just enough money based on an appraised value.

Furniture

Personal properties such as chandeliers, patio furniture, cabinets, and window treatments are also up for grabs. If the seller has a lot of furniture in the property and the buyer happens to want to keep them, then negotiation may ensue. Whatever's not included in the deal has to be stated once the contract is finalized. Otherwise, more negotiations may ensue.

Appliances

There are some appliances that may come with the property. These include built-in appliances like dishwasher, stove, and microwave. These appliances are a good tool for bumping up the value of the property and play a good role in negotiation.

5.2 Understanding A Motivated Seller and How to Add Value to A Deal

Real estate investments for commercial purposes can be categorized depending on the kind of deals used on them. These categories are the following:

CORE

Because they normally target stabilized, secured investments on the market, the core investments are known to be the least risky option. These include properties that have long-term leases on them rented by tenants with high credit score and properties that are located in extremely in-demand locations. These buildings are usually well kept and need little to no improvements for the new owner. So, as expected, these real estate properties don't experience great appreciation in value but instead offer steady income and very low to no risk at all.

This form of investment is perfect for investors who need capital preservation and long hold periods and usually allows for low leverage attainments. While Core investments are seemingly not as popular as the commercial real estate options, many people still choose them due to the low risk they offer.

Even though this form of investment is typically not as liquid as securities offered on an exchange in commercial real estate, they're usually considered the most liquid assets when it comes to opportunistic value addition projects since they're attractive, steady, and highly in-demand assets.

VALUE-ADD

Value-add commercial real estate investments is a form of investment that usually focuses on properties that aspire to increase their cash flow despite having in-place cash flow. This is done by making improvements on the property. This could mean doing some sort of physical improvements on the property that can justify the higher rent. But this must also intend to improve the standard of living of the people renting the property. When the property's net income was successfully improved by the operator, the next step is to sell the asset to get the ensuing appreciation in value.

OPPORTUNISTIC

The last in the list is the opportunistic investing. This form of investment involves investing in misjudged and extremely undervalued properties. These are the properties that require a lot of work to reach their full potential market value.

With this type of investment, your goal as an investor is to take a tactical risk to attain out-sized revenues. For this reason, there are many forms of asset investments that come under this category, which includes ground-up developments and emerging and adaptive markets. Opportunistic investments can also be the acquisition of foreclosed properties from banks.

If you choose to invest into this route, you'll need to think in advance and depend on the future of the asset because the returns will come from imminent rental income or the sale the property when the market gets better.

5.3 How to Approach People and Establish Credibility

There are a lot of traits that can help you become successful in this trade. But one of the most important things you need to improve about yourself is your ability to be credible in the eyes of others.

In some ways, your credibility is a higher bar compared to your success. This means that other people look at you as a dependable decision-maker and resource. This will allow others to rely on you because they know they can count on you when they need to trust their business to someone.

Being credible means developing a set of specific qualities – regardless of your role, industry, and organization. Here are some things you need to do if you're serious about being a credible businessman:

❖ **Be reliable.** In order to cultivate credibility, it's important to build trust, earn it, and use it. If people trust you, they wouldn't have a second thought about doing business with you. Remember that in the world of business, there's nothing more important than being trusted by people.

❖ **Be capable.** Be the master of your craft and show people that you are capable of actually doing things that you promised. Be confident and trust your skills, and when people see that, they will follow.

❖ **Be consistent.** Always be consistent in everything you do, say, and think. Show the people that everything you do matches everything you say. Without consistency inside and out, credibility wouldn't happen.

❖ **Be real.** To cultivate credibility, being genuine is necessary; when you are trying to gain trust, you cannot depend on the "fake it till you make it" approach. To be able to successfully establish your credibility, you should be ready for everything that may come your way.

❖ **Be sincere.** Sincerity also plays a huge part. This does not mean saying everything you have in your head but being truthful with everything you say. Practice doing more instead of talking more. Sincerity involves dedication and commitment and the willingness to be unwavering, straightforward, and unmovable.

❖ **Be respectful.** Showing people how you respect their feelings and opinions will mean a lot to them. So, make sure to treat everyone with respect – not because you're expecting something in return, but because that's how it should be.

❖ **Be responsible.** Being responsible with all your words and actions is one of the keys to being credible. It's also important that you accept that you commit mistakes and you show that you don't have a problem doing anything to fix any mistakes you make. If you're not sure of something, then let people know.

❖ **Be loyal.** Being able to learn how to show loyalty to people around you is one of the best ways to earn credibility. Keep in mind that loyalty is a mutual commitment, and you must always be willing to show it.

❖ **Be truthful.** Developing your reputation is a huge part of establishing credibility. Learn how to speak with openness and honesty. You must learn how to be transparent and genuine.

❖ **Be righteous.** Accept yourself and stop comparing yourself to others – be the righteous person who stands tall to honour the values you believe in. Always try to improve yourself to be a better version of you.

Chapter 6

Raising Finance

Any businessman who is just starting out would attest that gathering funds for a new business venture could be one of the most challenging parts of starting a business. No matter how passionate and eager you are about the business you are trying to start up, without enough funds, it will almost always be nothing.

While searching for an investor is definitely possible, this is not always the best option. Each of us has different situations, so what might work for others might not be a feasible option for you. Here are ways you can use to raise finance.

6.1 If You Have Bad Credit Score

It's true that finding money to start a business is not easy if you have a bad credit score. However, you have to know that this is not impossible. Here are some alternative ways you can follow in order to gather the money you need to start your real estate business.

1. Look beyond bank loans and credit cards. Studies reveal that credit card and bank financing account for only 25% of the total funding requirements of start-up businessmen. This statistic should give you some ease since it suggests that most of the money you need can originate from other resources.

It's possible to find lending agencies that target people with low credit score, but of course, there's always a catch – you can expect that they will charge you higher interest rate. A bank option for people with poor credit scores is a home equity line of credit, although I would be careful about putting my home on the line to fund a risky early-stage endeavour.

2. Borrow from people you know. Did you know that about 50% of the business is funded by people who borrowed money from people they know? These people they know are usually their friends and relative. If you're lucky, your family and friends might trust you enough to lend you some money. They might not even care if you have a poor credit score. If they think you are reliable and that you are capable of being successful in the business you are trying to get into, they might overlook your financial situation.

3. Seek microlenders and online lenders. It's not hard to find nonbank lenders online that are offering microloans to businessmen. These loans usually offer between $5,000 and $25,000. Not only these companies are willing to lend you money, but your payments to them will also be reported to credit bureaus, which means paying them can actually help you rebuild your credit scores. However, make sure to not go to the first one you find. You can always compare the interest rates to find and also read the fine prints.

Because of the benefits they offer, you can expect that they apply higher interest rates than your typical lending companies. For comparison, the average rate on business loans from friends and relative is currently at 7.6%, while the rate was over 12% - 20% at these establishments.

6.2 When You're Unemployed

Unemployment shouldn't stop you from dreaming big. Unlike when you just have a poor credit score, it is hard to find funds for your business when you are unemployed.

Unemployment does not necessarily mean you don't have a chance when it comes to acquiring a loan. While it sounds too good to be true, it's actually possible for someone who doesn't have a job to finance the business they are dreaming of.

What Lenders Seek from Personal Loan Applicants

Of course, when you are applying for a loan, you'll have to go through some sort of screening in order for the lender to know whether you are qualified for the loan or not. Here are some of the things the lender will look at when you are applying for a loan:

❖ **Income:** The most important thing for a lender is to know whether or not you are capable of paying them back. And to know that, they must look through your source of income.

❖ **Credit**: The lender is going to pull your credit file to see your credit score, payment history, as well as utilization.

❖ **Debt-to-income ratio**: They will also check whether or not you have other existing loans. If you happen to have other loans, they will see if your current income can handle the additional loan.

Income is an important part of getting a loan, and that could be a problem when you don't have a job. What you might not have realized is that income from a job is not your only option.

6.3 Alternative Forms of Income

In order to qualify for a personal loan, you will have to show that you have some form of consistent income. Without that, the lender is not likely to grant the loan.

Even though you don't have a job, you can still have other forms of income. Here are some of the options you can use.

- ❖ **Unemployment benefits:** If you're qualified for an unemployment benefit, that still counts as a source of income.

- ❖ **Freelance income**: All forms of income you earn from doing freelancing can count as a source of income.

- ❖ **Investment income**: Another source of income that many people overlook is the money you get from any existing investment.

You have to remember that regardless of which option you have, the lender will most likely perform some sort of income verification.

If you have already applied for a new job and waiting for you to start, that's also a good sign for the lenders that indicate that you can actually afford to pay for the loan. So, if you have a pending contract or certificate of being hired, you can inform the lender about it.

How to Apply for A Loan if You are Unemployed

1. Know your source of income

When applying for a loan, the first thing you have to do is to gather all the documents that explain your current source of income. As mentioned earlier, this could come in the form of other business, existing investments, freelance jobs, or a pending job. You have to prove that you have consisting earnings.

2. Protect your credit

The worst step is to do things that may cause your credit score to drop before you even get approved for a personal loan. This will surely affect your chances of approval as well as your interest rate. In order to protect your credit, see to it that you continue paying all your bills before you hit the due date. Don't rack up big balances on any of your credit cards, as it will increase your debt-to-income ratio and getting approved for a loan will be more difficult for you.

3. Find the right lender for you

There are two important things to look out for when searching for a lender that suits your needs:

- ❖ **Credit score requirements**: Again, there are different types of lenders, and not all of them require applicants to have a soaring credit score. If you have a good credit score, then good! If not, find the ones that don't grant people with a poor credit score.

- ❖ **Amounts offered**: Know how much you need and find a lender that will offer the amount of money you need to start up your business. They will tell you their minimum and maximum, so see if they match up your requirements.

Other Financing Options When You're Unemployed

Get a consignee: By having a consignee on your loan application, the lender is going to check the credit score and income of that person. It will work as if the consignee is also applying for the loan.

Because a consignee is also responsible for the loan the same as the person who borrowed it, most people are hesitant to be one. But then again, it's not impossible to make people agree to be your consignee. You can ask your parents, relatives, or friends to do it for you. They won't hesitate if they know that you are capable of paying the money back.

Credit cards: Credit cards generally are not what you would use to carry a balance due to their interest rates. 0% APR credit cards are a great exception, as they let you pay 0 interest for as long as the intro period of the card lasts. Throughout that time, you just have to make minimum payments. It's also not impossible to find credit companies that wouldn't charge you high-interest fees.

If ever you already applied for a low-interest credit card, this option would be a smart way to pay them off when you don't have a job yet.

Use the equity in your home: Another option could be to refinance your current home and pull out as much equity out of the property as possible. People see this as a bad thing, but not when you're using the money to invest in further assets for cashflow that can pay for your cost of living. Most people are in a rush to pay off their home and be debt-free. But this just leaves them penny less afterwards and still needing to pay bills etc.

Chapter 7

ADDING VALUE TO A PROPERTY

There are people who would buy homes and fall in love with them just the way they are. They would choose not to change anything and keep them the same way. It's different for others though. For them, buying a property is an opportunity. They choose to buy the property, not due to the way it looks or the current features of the house. They choose to buy it because they can see its full potential. They probably had imagined what it would look like when the kitchen was changed or when they put a different kind of sofa in the living room. They already planned the add-ons and changes they want to make in order to make the home more valuable, inviting, and profitable.

This is a good way of thinking for homebuyers, especially those who have the intention of using it as a business investment. First of all, the house would have an improvement that could expand the overall beauty of the place. What used to be just a small piece of land could turn into a pleasing home with many features and amazing landscaping. Regardless of its size, it would have the appeal that future buyers will actually fall in love with. Another advantage is that it would increase the overall value of the property. And the higher the value the property has, the more equity it has and the more money the owner can get when it is used for business purposes. And last of all, the house would have better functionality, and you are able to use it for a long time, especially if you're not planning on reselling it.

Therefore, home improvements would always be a smart idea. But you have to know that it's important to choose the right kind of project that is ideal for your home. Here are different ways to add value to your property:

1. Make it look more appealing

Starting from the outside all the way to the inside, your home should look appealing. The exterior of the property has to make a potential client want to see what's inside. You have to keep the landscaping presentable by keeping it well-maintained. If the yard looks dull compared to the houses next to it, you may want to consider repainting the fences and the door and adding flowers.

When the exterior looks better, you can then move on to the bathroom and kitchen. It's hard to reach your property's highest value if you don't pay enough attention to these two rooms.

And there's no need to invest in heated towel racks or marble floors as well. A small kitchen remodelling adds about 80% of its cost in added value averagely.

The same thing goes for the bathrooms; a midrange remodel – adding new flooring and some updated fixtures add about 70% ROI, while an upscale bathroom remodel attracts about 56% on average.

2. Make it low-maintenance

Because a lot of home buyers are anxious about purchasing a home that will require endless maintenance, replacing a huge component before putting it up for sale or rent might calm fears of an emergency repair in the near future and assist you in getting higher ROI.

Making things easier to clean and maintain can also help you boost the value of the property. You may want to get a new carpet and replace old materials with new ones that don't require much maintenance.

3. Make it more efficient and eco-friendly

The property can have more value to the eyes of the buyers if they can help them save money from energy consumption. You can apply for energy-efficient mortgages or EEMs, which allows you to borrow additional debt to help you upgrade the property and make it more energy-efficient. This kind of loan usually offers low-interest rates.

Properties, especially the ones that are located in places where it can get too hot or too cold, get more value if they have energy conservation features. Ask an expert how you can make the property more efficient, but some of the popular options you can turn to are replacing the windows with double-panel ones and using LED bulbs to illuminate the house at night.

If you want to go big, then you can consider adding a solar panel to your roof. Based on the survey performed by the National Association of Realtors on 39% of their realtors, solar panels increased professed property value. But because solar panels are a huge financial and structural commitment, this only makes sense if you want a long-term benefit from the property like if you are planning to get it rented and not a quick boost in resale value.

To make things clearer for you, you may want to schedule an assessment with a certified energy inspector or your utility company in order to know where your home is wasting energy and what type of upgrades are going to save you the most money.

4. Make it spacious

Square footage has a great effect on the value of a home. One of the main features of a property that indicates its value is its size.

Unsurprisingly, the bigger the property is, the more value is added to it. And even though you don't tell the potential buyer its actual size, this is something that can easily be caught by the eyes. Of course, you can't widen the size of the property unless you bought its surrounding lands, but one thing you can do is to make it spacious. You can add a patio if possible. Or clean up the basement and make it look liveable.

5. Make it smarter

Based on the 2018 survey by Coldwell Banker, safety-enhancing gadgets are on top of the list of "smart" technologies potential clients want in their new homes. These safe and smart devices include fire detectors, thermostats, carbon monoxide detectors, door locks, security cameras, and auto lighting.

While smart tech does not always increase the value of the home, it makes it more appealing. Tech-savvy individuals will be more than willing to pay more if they see how cutting-edge the features are. The good thing about this is that there is not a lot of handyman work involved in this – you only have to install the gadgets, and you are good to go.

7.1 House Flipping: 4 Key Factors that Affect the Costs

The cost to flip a house is equivalent to the sum of the costs of acquisition, repair, sales, and marketing. There are many factors that affect the costs of house flipping. But most of the time, the cost you need to incur to successfully flip a house is about 10% of the price you paid to buy the title of the property.

Again, the total costs to flip a house will greatly depend on the type of project. That is one of the reasons why flipping real estate is super appealing- it is feasible on almost any kind of budget. While it's impossible to tell exactly the amount to spend when flipping a house, there are 4 main expenses that involve this project. These four main expenses of flipping a house are:

Purchase Price of Fix and Flip Property

The property acquisition price is the total money you spent to get the house to your name. In these expenses, you also have to settle the property's purchase amount as well as the closing expenses associated with it. These are the expenses you pay at the settlement of a transaction.

The purchase price is the amount of money you pay to acquire a property. The total purchase price is the payment you make for property itself as well as the land where it is located, and the price depends on the type of property you are buying – if you are buying a condominium type property, then you don't have to pay for the land. The purchase price does not include insurance or taxes, but depending on how the deal is built, it might include custom window treatments, appliances, and light furniture.

There are two things you have to consider when buying a property.

1. The use of comparable properties to see if they match the type of property you are originally looking for; and

2. The costs of after-repair value or ARV.

If you're new to house flipping, calculating the costs can be a little confusing. So, if you want to make it easier, you can start by purchasing properties that only require cosmetic repairs. Dealing with this kind of properties is easier.

Fix & Flip Property Closing Costs

You're the one who's responsible for the closing costs when you buy a property you intend to flip. These expenses will include the transfer taxes, property insurance, share of property taxes, title insurance, as well as the title company fees. The financing would have its own expenses at closing as well if you're the one who's financing the purchase. Both the lender and the real estate agent may offer you a breakdown of the closing expenses.

A conservative rule of thumb is that the closing costs of the buyer will be 5% of the purchase price of the property. If you bought a property amounting $300,000, expect to pay around 5% of $300,000, which is $15,000. So, the $300,000 property will now cost you $315,000. It's important to not forget to include them when trying to calculate the total costs of buying a house to flip because these costs will significantly affect the ROI

Also, it's always a good idea to take photos of the property in its original state and afterwards to give to the valuer of the property to show what you've done. This can help as a valuer may sometimes go away and actually forget your property if they've viewed many others on that day or week.

Cost to Rehab a Property

The cost to rehab a property differs depending on how critical the changes are that need to be done, the size of the property, as well as how much the labour would be. The costs of the rehab include both labour and materials needed.

Fix and Flip Material + Labour Expenses

Don't forget to include delivery costs and construction fees if you had to hire a person to do the job when calculating the total costs of the materials for the project.

The expenses you need to settle on the materials will vary greatly depending on the scope of the rehab project, but they largely fall into two categories:

- ❖ Appliances: Common appliances like a stove, HVAC, refrigerator, etc.

- ❖ Building Materials: The common materials for building a house like paint, nails, etc.

Make sure to also add the labour to make the project possible. They are going to charge you to install all of the materials you bought. There are contractors that charge per hour, but there are also ones that charge per project. This is something you can negotiate for the price and put into a signed contract before the work starts. You might have to hire different labourers depending on your specific needs.

Common labourers include:

- ❖ Day labourers or handymen
- ❖ Electrician
- ❖ General contractor (GC)
- ❖ Landscapers
- ❖ Painters
- ❖ Plumber

The extent of the rehab for the property is the main determining factor on how much it would cost you to flip a house. Again, it's best for beginners to choose properties that only require cosmetic repairs. When you do it successfully, the next projects are going to be easier, and you can eventually choose properties that might have more complicated requirements.

Cosmetic Home Repairs for a Fix & Flip Costs

Cosmetic repairs for the property are minor repairs and improvements that are required to increase the value of the property. You can definitely boost the property's value if you did things right. The faster the project finishes, the lower the costs would be. Labour and material expenses are also lower. But because the property is already in better condition than it was before, you can expect the acquisition costs to be higher.

Chapter 8

Common Mistakes When Starting Real Estate Business

There are many things to consider when investing in real estate, but the first important thing to know are the mistakes to avoid on this endeavour. You will want to try to avoid these common mistakes, and you will also want to make sure that you know the important things to do when you're involved in commercial real estate investing. Yes, committing mistakes is almost inevitable, but the more you prepare yourself for it, the more likely it is for you to avoid them.

Mistake #1 - Ignoring the Condition of Your Local Market

One of the major mistakes one can make in commercial real estate investing is to ignore the conditions of the local market. Even though you're investing in a great property, if you choose to do it in a bad market, you are still likely to lose money. On the other hand, a bad property can potentially generate a lot of money if it's within the right area, so demand is always a key factor to remember.

Mistake #2 - Not Doing Proper Due Diligence

Another common mistake that many new investors make when it comes to commercial real estate investing is not taking the time to perform proper due diligence. It can be a good idea to find people that have done similar projects in the area as to the one you're working in. Places like Facebook groups can be a great place to start to find these sort of people.

Mistake #3 - Borrowing Too Much

This is one of the main reasons why an investment business fails. Borrowing more money than you should is a mistake that will certainly lead you to the pit of disaster. You must avoid borrowing too much money unless you are 100% sure that the ROI can afford it within the right timeframe or if you know you have the money to pay for it. Keep in mind that when you invest, you at least have to breakeven, or you will lose money. Of course, your goal is to make sure that you actually generate money on the investment.

Mistake #4 - Not Having Good Plan B, C, and D

A lot of people have found out it out the hard way that you must have a plan B or just an exit plan in case things go south. Make sure that you have strategies for exiting in different unlikable situations. Without multiple exit plans, you might end up being stuck somewhere you don't want to be. It's always a good rule of thumb to imagine the worst-case scenario before getting into a deal and work from there.

Mistake #5 - Doing Business with Bad Partners

While most of the problems you might have to deal with have something to do with the property itself, people could also be your main problem. By partnering with someone who you don't get along with, you are already dealing with a disaster. It's best to get out of that partnership if you see that it's not working out from the beginning. Otherwise, it's just going to be a complete disaster.

Mistake #6 - Taking Too Many Risks

Taking risk is a part of getting into a business. However, there is a fine line between good risk and unhealthy risk. You want to avoid what is called "overreaching" where you go all out on taking risks. Yeah, big deals might probably come at you, but make sure it's something you can realistically deal with.

Learn to crawl before you can run.

Mistake #7 - Owning More Land Than Money

A lot of investors have found themselves committing the mistake of owning more land than they have money to actually cover. If you have a lot of properties at the same time and you are trying to use the gains you get for one to cover what you're losing on another, then you're not doing this business right – you just set yourself on a never-ending cycle. Escape the problem properties right away, even though it might seem difficult. Then, take all of your time and focus on the properties that are going to let you make the maximum amount of earning.

These are all common mistakes. Do yourself a favour and try to avoid them at all costs. However, it's important that you remember that even though you accidentally make a mistake and get yourself in a situation that you didn't want to be in, you can still always fix it and go the right way.

8.1 Things to Do to Prevent Mistakes

While mistakes are inevitable, there are things you can do to prevent them. Here are smart things you can do to avoid common real estate investment mistakes.

❖ **Always Investigate the Deal**

Before closing a commercial real estate deal, it's important to take your time to do some sort of investigation on the deal. This will mean that you need to take the time to do due diligence about any type of property that you're thinking of buying. It's not very smart to get into investing without doing your due diligence – you are likely to end up with a bad deal. Always remember to invest with formulas, not feelings. ROI and areas with demand are key.

❖ Learn from the Mistakes of Others

Learn from people; if you don't know anything, just ask. Like we have said previously, this business model has a great blueprint to learn from. It might involve a lot of test runs, but always try to find out from people that have done what you're about to do. "A smart man learns from his mistakes. A wise man learns from others' mistakes".

❖ Figure Out How Long You Can Wait for a Pay-out

You will have to make sure that you know how long you are able to wait before you actually get a pay-out on the investment you're making. Make sure you have a realistic estimation of how long you can really wait, or you might just end up facing cashflow problems. In time, multiple investments will cover this problem.

Chapter 9

HOW TO MANAGE PROPERTIES

A lot of people think that finding a good deal is the hardest part of investing in real estate. They spend long hours seeking and dealing for the right property. They crunch the numbers over and over again. They make calls over and over again, and walk through a lot of basements and attics. They set their hopes up and then rushed within the same 24 hours. They check the neighbourhood and do their research, check, and then double-check market values. They write up offers, a lot of them with low, almost silly prices. After a lot of hours spent, sacrifices made, offers countered, and displaying much persistence, they have an offer accepted. Now the real work begins.

Step 1: Buy & Repair

Buying the property and getting into good repair is the first step of managing an investment or rental property. Before you open up the property for rentals, there are two important things you have to work on first. The focus of your priority should go to choosing the right property to buy and how you can make it profitable by repairing it.

Step 2: Setting Prices and Expectations

Having control over the rental property and feeling ready to start out the business is not enough to get started. Before you find the tenant who will stay in your property, there's one more important thing you need to get to. And that is to figure out how much you are going to charge for the property and what your expectations are from people who are staying there.

Market Research in Area

You must do your research first before deciding on the rent. Find out the demand for rental properties in the area and know how much is the average rent there.

Although you probably have idea what the answers to these questions are after searching for the property there, doing another round of research would be better.

Know the answers to these questions:

- ❖ How much is the average income in the area?

- ❖ What's the average size of the family?

- ❖ What's the average price of the rental?

- ❖ Does the location have any extra-special benefits that you are able to charge more for?

As you know more information about the other rentals on the market as well as the going rates, you can suitably price your rental property.

Tenant Requirements

On top of figuring out the amount to charge to your tenant, another important thing you must figure out is the requirements you have to set for your tenants. You'd have a better opportunity to find high-quality tenants if you determined the requirements you need to look out for.

Here are some things a landlord can ask from the potential tenant:

- ❖ Credit score minimum

- ❖ Employment requirement

- ❖ Minimum income

- ❖ Character reference

- ❖ Previous rental history

- ❖ Smoker or not?

Step 3: Rent Your Property

Now, let's get on the most challenging, yet the most exciting part of the rental process. Now you're ready to hunt for the right tenants you'll take into your property.

Advertising

Advertising your property is another important part of the whole business process – in fact, this is essential regardless of what type of business you have. Advertise anywhere you can; you can invest some money for additional exposure – it's always going to be worth it. You can use popular home sites such as Trulia and Zillow to help you advertise your property.

Finding Quality Tenants

It's important to not accept any tenant who inquires about the property. Make sure that you are renting your property to a high-quality tenant.

So, how can you determine whether the tenant is good or not? A good tenant is someone who pays on time, respects your property, and doesn't cause troubles. Of course, you wouldn't know whether or not an applicant is a good or a bad tenant by simply interviewing them, but as you do this more, reading tenants would be easier over time.

You can make use of a rental questionnaire that will surely help you learn if every prospective tenant is a great fit. You must, however, be sensitive about the things you will ask the applicants. You don't want to ask them about their personal lives, beliefs, and political preferences. In order to find a good tenant, you have to do the following:

- ❖ Know where they work and how much they earn
- ❖ Perform a background and credit check
- ❖ Ask for their references
- ❖ Call their former landlords
- ❖ Interview them face-to-to

Even though you do all of these things, you may miss something that specifies a bad tenant. Since screening tenants could be pretty tricky, it might be a good idea to hire a third-party tenant screening service that will help you analyse all gathered information to meet the best tenants.

Writing and Reviewing Rental Contracts

When you find a good tenant for your property, it is going to be time to sign the rental contract. If you have no idea how to make a contract, you can find existing contracts online that you can use as a reference.

Otherwise, you can always get help from a real estate agent or a lawyer that will make sure that you wouldn't be missing any details on the paper. From there, you are able to work by yourself. Don't forget to put details regarding rental payment schedule, maintenance information, eviction process, and home rules within the contract. Furthermore, you have to make sure that you disclose and gather a security deposit when you are the agreement.

Review the Contract

Reread the contract again before presenting it to the new tenant, and again, reread it together with the tenant. Make sure that the tenant reads and understands what's written on the contract. Also, give him a chance to ask questions, or if he has confusions, be ready to answer him clearly.

Walking Through the Property

Before making it official, you can have a final check on everything with your new tenant. Explain everything and document all the details you can possibly note.

With these details, you can be sure that you have proof that everything was well before the tenant came in. This is useful in case there are some sort of disagreements in the future over damages or other issues.

Step 4: Checking and Maintenance

Once the new tenant has moved into the property, you might think that you no longer have a responsibility over the property during the time of his stay. Well, this is not always the case if you're a responsible landlord. Because that property is still considered yours, you'll be the person to call in case a problem occurs. If something goes wrong with anything in the house, you'll be the one to fix it. For example, if the heater suddenly stops working, then you're the one responsible for getting it fixed.

Rental Visits

It's very beneficial to make a scheduled visit to the property at least every 6 months.

You can visit them after a few months of them staying in to make sure that there's no problem with the place. This will also make the tenant feel that you are open to hearing anything as some tenants tend to be too shy to disturb the landlord. There might be small problems popping up that they had not yet reported to you; these walkthroughs are the best time to get some more insight.

On top of seeing how they are doing, doing a visit also helps you make sure that your property is being respected by its tenants. By making the tenant know that you do regular visits to the property, they will be more likely to take care of the property even more.

Regular Maintenance

Every property requires some sort of maintenance. When small problems pop out, like plumbing or heater problems, your tenants will be more likely to contact you. And of course, they also expect you to take action immediately to fix them.

To do the maintenance faster, you must prepare yourself in advance:

❖ List of reliable local workers

❖ Contact information for local landlords who can help

❖ List of basic repair problems that you can fix your own

❖ Specific maintenance fund

❖ Set schedule for regular check-ups of appliances, especially the AC and heaters

Big Repairs

While all landlords hope that it wouldn't happen, there's always the chance that you'll have to take on a huge repair while you're getting the property rented out. There might be big problems that happen to the property. These problems might be due to natural disasters like flooding or tornado.

If the property requires an important repair that is going to force your tenant to get out of the property for a few days, it's your responsibility to give them housing during that period because they already paid. As the property owner, you should be responsible for where they are going to spend the nights while the property is being fixed, whether it means renting a hotel for them.

If ever something very serious happens to the house that it becomes impossible for anyone to live there, you have to talk to the tenant and tell them that the lease contract might have to be ended earlier. So, make sure to mention on your contract that in case of critical damage on the property due to damage caused by natural disaster or unforeseen event, the contract might get terminated.

Step 5: Collecting Rent

One of the most important jobs of a landlord is to collect the rent! Each landlord has a different preference for collecting rent. Some still pay in checks or some may use electronic banking or online payment systems like PayPal and Venmo.

Each method may come with its own pros and cons, but ultimately, it all depends on you which one you think is most convenient. If you choose the online system, however, you have to keep in mind that it might deduct some fee, so make sure to work this out with your tenant.

Raising Rent

Because of the rising expenses in the area, it might come to a point when you have to raise your rent. Although it might sound impossible to raise the rent while an existing tenant lives there, this thing happens more often than you think. So, in the contract, make sure to state the possibility of raising the rent. It's up to them whether they still want to stay at the property or look for somewhere else to live.

Late Fees

Make sure to apply a late fee for all the renters who didn't pay their dues on time. If the tenant is always late when paying their rents, make sure that they know the possibility of eviction if they keep resisting to pay on time.

Tenants are going to come up with all the excuses in the book for their late payments, and being empathetic about their situation is okay. However, when a tenant starts to consecutively pay their rent very late, it is a sign that they might no longer be able to afford your property.

By enforcing a clear policy regarding late fees, you are going to have peace of mind that they are going to avoid paying their rent late.

The late fees policy must be made clear in the rental agreement. Don't forget to include relevant parts of the contract as a reference when giving them the notice of late payment. It should be clear to them that possible eviction may happen.

Step 6: Evictions

No landlord ever wants to be in a position where they want to evict people, but this is something that happens constantly. As a new landlord, you probably don't have any idea what to do when you get into such a situation, and it's okay. To make sure that you're following the local laws, doing research beforehand would be necessary.

The eviction process might involve a whole court process if the tenant refuses to leave. The whole process can be a little bit frustrating, but it's very important to follow the legal process to avoid any possible trouble.

Any form of an attempt to evict the tenant yourself can be considered a criminal offence. In order to avoid trouble, here are some of the basic steps you may need to follow:

- ❖ Send them the official notice, which states the deadline until when they could fix the issue that breaches the agreement.

- ❖ If the conditions are not met, file the eviction with the court.

- ❖ When filing for eviction, don't accept any form of payment from the tenant. Doing so may invalidate the process of eviction.

- ❖ Be aware of the local laws to make sure that you're not breaking any rules.

- ❖ You may want to hire a lawyer if you find the law confusing.

❖ Wait for the court ruling and local sheriff to do the actual eviction.

Step 7: Accounting

Accounting and tax management is something that is very important, but you might not be good at it. Fortunately, you can always hire a property manager to help you. If you had a property management company, they're going to produce this information in reports for you, but doing it by yourself can be quite complicated.

To make the business accounting easier, here are some tips you may want to follow.

1. You can hire an accountant to do the taxing for you; the cost is worth it. They are going to help you maximize deductions and guarantee a clean record.

2. The money spent on maintenance and other basic property maintenance should be clearly documented.

3. To avoid confusion, you may want to have separate bank accounts for your business expenses.

4. Save money that will cover taxes and other fees that you may find surprising.

Becoming a Property Manager

Becoming a good rental manager is a responsibility you may want to master! While you can always hire someone to do this, doing it yourself will save you a lot of money. And after all, it's not that complicated.

Keep in mind that in its most minimalistic form, property management needs only some simple steps:

- ❖ Purchase and repair a property
- ❖ Set up rental expenses and tenant requirement
- ❖ Search for tenants and rent the house to them
- ❖ Maintain the property
- ❖ Collect rent and pay taxes
- ❖ Enjoy the profit!

Managing a property can be overwhelming, especially for beginners, but this shouldn't be the case. When done properly using the knowledge you acquire as you research on this field, you will be rewarded not only with monetary wealth but also with the satisfaction that you are able to manage such a complicated task.

9.1 Different Ways You Can Advertise Your Rental Property

Getting your rental filled is of main concern when you're turning over rental units. Landlords know that a vacant unit equals to lost profits. That's why having a good marketing strategy is so extremely important. Just filling the unit isn't enough; smart landlords see the marketing effort as the first step to screen the tenants. A good marketing campaign is the best method for landlords to lower the risk of picking the best person to rent the unit. They would like to make sure that the person they choose can pay rent on time and accomplish the responsibilities of the lease. Having to pick a marginal tenant due to lack of options can prove to be expensive. The cost evictions, turnover, maintenance, and repairs can be pretty overwhelming.

❖ The best and easiest means to advertise your rental home is the time-tested "For Rent" sign. As simple as it may look like, this means capitalizes on the idea that renters are going to drive around desired communities seeking future housing.

In order to improve visibility, it's recommended that a sign be placed on the property. A lot of landlords put a small box on one of the signs to place flyers with rental information. This will let the landlord disqualify prospects by revealing price, expectations, and policy. Qualifying prospects are going to save much time by cutting pointless showings and phone calls.

Signs should reveal contact information visibly and should be written in big print. A lot of landlords lose rental opportunities by making the writing extremely small or hard to read. Make sure that the sign will attract the eyes of everyone who will pass by. You can make it extra attractive by adding two balloons next to the sign.

❖ The second most efficient advertising method is to distribute the rental details flyer to every free community bulletin board in the area. You can find these boards at public places like churches, grocery stores, community centres, as well as government offices.

Be ready and put announcements or flyers about the availability of your rental property on bulletin boards in the area. This way is especially effective if you're marketing to college students and immigrants.

- ❖ Another effective way is asking people to endorse your rental property and giving them commission once they successfully find it. Customary referral rewards range from $50 to $200. This is effective and always works faster.

- ❖ Another classic yet effective way is making the most of classified ads in newspapers. They could be more expensive if you choose newspapers in most cities. However, you can simply choose a smaller local newspaper as they are cheaper. Ads in big newspapers are usually extremely short since word usage is limited. Smaller publications let more information in the ad.

- ❖ Now, for the most effective way of advertising – using online ads. Everyone is online now. You can put your ads on Facebook or Craigslist, and you'll surely be flooded with inquiries about your property. By using the internet, you don't have to worry about only adding limited words on the ads. You can write as many details as you want and you can also upload pictures in order for potential tenants to have a vision of what the unit looks like even without visiting the property in person.

9.2 How to Get the Best Tenants

Choosing a tenant can be a complicated process, but it doesn't have to be. There are landlords who tend to be relaxed about this process, and it's mostly because they've done this several times, and they already know that they are doing. Even though there's no sure-fire way for you to know everything about the tenant, there are several ways to have a better understanding of the tenant before you accept them to live in your property. Here are important things you must always remember.

Pay heed to the overall presentation of the possible tenant

Of course, every landlord should act in accordance with Fair Housing rules and laws. But then again, it's possible for landlords to consider the overall presentation of the potential tenant. The tenant's sex, age, or race doesn't have to do with it, but rather the overall presentation for the first impression such as the way they dress, talk, and carry themselves.

Perform a credit check

A credit check might require a fee on the part of the tenant or the owner, depending on which state they are in. A credit check is going to give a record of how the tenant has settled his previous financial responsibilities. This is going to include information about collections, late payments, and delinquencies. In today's age, the economy has been pretty unstable, so always keep in mind that if the prospective tenant has any type of financial problem. Most tenants usually have some kind of flaw, so don't expect anyone to be a perfect person.

Actually, your main worry should be to know as to whether or not the tenant is able to pay his rent or not.

Perform a background check

A background check can be performed through an organization for a small fee, and it's definitely worth it. A background check usually involves checking of lawsuits, criminal record, and other public information that proves that the potential tenant is not a threat. Again, no one is perfect, and one flaw shouldn't make them disqualified to be your tenant. But if you see that they have recorded offences such as sexual assault, robbery, and domestic violence, then you should avoid accepting them.

Make a high-quality application as well as a lease agreement

You might want to ask help from a legal expert to create a professional and high-quality application and lease agreement. This document is crucial as it explains your expectations and your role as a landlord. This document is going to be your protection in case things go wrong with your tenant, so the little fee you might spend is definitely worth it.

Keep a fair screening process

As a landlord, it's important to keep a fair screening process for possible tenants. So, you have to make sure that every decision you make is based on business online and not any personal information. That's why I discourage landlords to ask their potential tenants about their religion, sexual orientation, political beliefs, and other things that could lead to disagreement.

Tenant interview

Doing a brief interview with a potential tenant is a good way to get to know them and know their needs and expectations. Don't say anything that could be interpreted as discrimination, but it's okay to ask about whether they have pets, how many people are going to stay in the unit, and whether they are a smoker or not.

The truth is that there's always a risk, and you cannot guarantee how the tenant will act when they finally move into your place. Only because a tenant looks a certain way, it doesn't mean that he's going to be a good or bad tenant. The best thing a landlord could do is use the options at their disposal such as background checks, credit checks, and interviews in order to develop a complete picture of the tenant before they move in.

9.3 How to Protect Yourself from Bad Tenants

Hoarding, late payments, unauthorized roommates, and illegal activities – tenant problems come in different sizes, shapes, and forms, and the severity differs from each other. Even with the most severe process of screening and property rules in place, if you're a landlord, you're likely to deal with these things at some point in your life. With any problems, however, being professional is a must and will definitely take you a long way: Communicate clearly and immediately, and take the important steps – regardless of how complicated they may be – to keep a safe and lucrative rental.

Now, in this subchapter, we're going to talk about the proper ways how you can handle common problems tenants face and lease violations they commit. The key to dealing with tenants that are pretty difficult is to document everything. Each state has different laws, so again, make sure to ask a legal professional for advice on what to do when a problem with tenants arises.

Okay, so you're having trouble with your tenant...

Perhaps, he's not paying the rent on time for the last few weeks. Or the neighbours have been contacting you that your tenants are making noise at late hours. Maybe complaints of loud music and foul smell have begun flooding in. It's best to set your emotions aside the moment you feel like a problem is starting to arise. When a problem arises, remember that there are only two possible outcomes – it's either the tenant fixes the problem, or he leaves. There are few things to remember before you get on justifying a problem with your tenant.

❖ Know the law

Every state follows its own laws and ordinances. As a landlord, it's your responsibility to know the laws, rights, and all the responsibilities that go with being a property owner. Again, if you need to know more, don't be afraid to contact an attorney.

❖ Follow the policies and processes

The moment the tenant signs the contract, it means that they are ready to follow your terms, rules, and policies in running the property. Ask the tenant if they have further questions regarding the rules you apply and give them the copy so they can read it again later on.

The lease agreement must explain what tenants are allowed and not allowed to do with the property, the amount they need to pay, when is it due, and how it is going to be paid. On top of it, it's important to include rules about noise, resident-to-resident argument resolution, landlord responsibilities, tenant responsibilities, guidelines on additional occupants, pets, guests, smoking, maintenance of the property, and normal deterioration.

❖ Document everything

As mentioned earlier, this is the most important thing you could do for yourself as a landlord. Document the policies and procedures for dealing with the problem or complaint of the tenant, which includes expected response times, types of communication, notices, warnings, and when to escalate the problem. Sometimes, a meeting is needed where you can discuss the incident reports and perform incident reviews with your team in a meeting. You might also want to make incident reports and conduct incident review meetings with the tenants and your team.

❖ Get training

If you hire a staff to help you manage your business, then you have to make sure they are fully familiar with the whole processes and policies, that know your policies and procedures, and that they know the different types of tenant warnings, termination notices, as well as incident reports. When the tenant is emotional, getting fired up is an easy thing as well. And no matter how disrespectful a tenant might be, keeping professionalism is something each of the members must practice all the time.

A respectful conversation with the tenant might be enough to stop the problem before it escalates. If ever a non-legal problem happens, you can call the tenant and ask if you can meet in person to discuss and fix the problem. Use your judgment because there are cases when help from the authorities might be needed. Be specific and direct when it comes to your discussion and highlight the problem and the consequences of not following the policies and rules. Rather than saying, "Let me know when you'll remove the trash," say, "Get rid of the trash by Sunday, otherwise, you'll have to pay a fine." By having a basic knowledge of these techniques and strategies, it's going to be easier for you to navigate a solution to the problem a tenant might be having.

❖ **It is not personal, so it shouldn't be**

As a landlord, it's possible for you to deal with tenants with some heart-breaking stories. It's okay to be understanding, but all in all, you must be firm and solid when it comes to sticking to your policies. You have these policies to protect you and your business. On top of it, this type of discussion should only be discussed between you and the tenant. Significant others or family members may want to get involved, but this should only be between you and your tenant.

❖ Treat your tenant with respect

There are some problems that are not easy to discuss with your tenant – some of these are late payment and hoarding. See to it that you treat problems with privacy, even though they are not technically confidential data. Be careful when sharing sensitive information with people who shouldn't be involved. Furthermore, if you set a schedule to meet up with the tenant to discuss something, make sure to show up there on time.

❖ Put safety first

If it happens that a certain situation is already putting anyone in danger, then don't wait and call the police right away. Although you want to apply professionalism at all times, you shouldn't risk anyone's safety in exchange for anything. Call the authorities right away when you suspect that your tenant is involved in anything illegal. When criminal charges are pressed, you can then carry on with eviction process.

❖ Notice of termination

As a landlord, you can use several kinds of warnings and notices. Familiarize yourself with the local laws to see how you can serve the notice, particularly when it is an eviction notice, and ensure that you are serving the right notice to deal with the issue.

These are 3 of the most common notices:

- ❖ **Non-payment of Rent Notice:** Use this in case a tenant fails to pay rent on time. It notifies the tenants to settle their payment within a specified amount of time, or they will be forcedly evicted.

❖ **Quit Notice:** This is used when a tenant violates a term or condition of the lease. The tenant should have a specific amount of time to fix the problem, or they are going to be forcedly evicted.

❖ **Vacate Notice:** This is used when a tenant causes serious, recurrent, or dangerous acts. The tenant doesn't have a chance to fix anything, and they need to leave.

Each of these notices must include these basic elements for them to be valid. Here are the specifics you may want to include when sending a notice:

❖ **The name and address of the tenant**

❖ **Information about the violation**

❖ **The number of days wherein the tenant should comply**

❖ **Signature and date**

Chapter 10

REAL ESTATE TAX & LEGALITIES

Every state in the US maintains a tax assessor's office. So, what is the tax assessor? This office is responsible for evaluating the value of all real estate set in the county. This is also the one that is responsible for keeping precise records of location and ownership. The tax assessor makes an assessment of a particular property, enters the assessment into the records and takes up or takes down the property tax by how much the price has gone up or went down. The office of the treasurer is going to collect the taxes, but the tax assessor is responsible for putting up the rate.

Property taxes can go up or go down based on two different variables: the amount owed and the rate. Tax rates that are going up but falling property values may lead to a lesser or greater amount owed. At the same time, rising property values and falling tax rates could have an equally indeterminate result when it comes to how much the homeowner needs to pay. The worst situation is a rising tax rate and rising property value. All in all, these taxes are one of the most troublesome features of homeownership. Homeowners should be mindful of the things they are able to do to raise or lower their taxes on the property.

A definite way to bring up the property tax amount owed is to add value to the property. Home improvement, cleaning up the yard, improving the looks of the curb, repainting the walls, just anything that could raise the value of the property can raise its tax liability. The fastest way to avoid this is just don't build. Alternatively, if a structural or cosmetic improvement should be made, the homeowner could consult the tax assessor's office beforehand.

A very simple way to lower property tax assessments is to go to assessor's office and ask for a copy of the property tax record. Mistakes, however, are very common. If you see a mistake on the record, the assessor has to, by law, make it right. Sometimes a whole re-evaluation may be in order, as mistakes on the part of the assessor can cost homeowners a lot in taxes.

Assessed values depend greatly on the home's exterior attractiveness. The appeal of the curb then plays a big role in the tax assessment. The tax assessor has many scopes when considering improvements to external features. Again, the best way to avoid this is to not to make improvements until the assessment is done. Or just don't do them at all if possible.

Make sure to let the assessor in whenever he wants to perform the assessment. If you deny him entrance, it may give him complete freedom to put the highest value possible to your property – so be nice. Unfortunately, this unconditional authority happens in most states in the United States.

10.1 How to Calculate Property Taxes

One of the most confusing things you might have to deal with as a real estate investor is calculating the taxes. But then again, this is something anyone can learn. This is especially the fact because even though calculations aren't always the same for all local governments, the same rules are normally followed.

The Assessment of the Property

The local tax assessor's office is the one who is going to determine the value of your property. Usually, this assessment is done annually or after every few years. This all depends on the law of the state or municipality. Before you can get your property tax bills, you are required to get value assessment first.

The assessment is derived from the estimation of the tax assessor based on the property's market value. The value may come in three different forms:

❖ **The cost method:** This is when the assessor calculates the total amount of the property if it was to be built from scratch. Of course, this varies based on how old the house is and where it is located.

❖ **Sales comparison:** The assessor will base the value of your property on other properties of the same type, size, and condition, located in the same area or town. He'll then adjust for variables that might make your property more or less valuable compared to others that were sold.

❖ **The income method:** This assessment is usually used in business and commercial properties. Here, the possible amount of income if the property were to be rented out is calculated.

Chapter 11

BUILDING AN ESSENTIAL TEAM

Building a real estate investing team is important in achieving massive success in real estate investments. Many of the best real estate investors are aware of the real value that a team could add. After all, it's going to be too difficult, if not, impossible, for you to do everything by yourself. And this is where the investing team comes into the picture.

What Is A Real Estate Investing Team?

A real estate investing team is a group of experts with whom to work closely with before, during, and after purchasing real estate investments. The real estate investing team helps with financing, sourcing deals, the process of due diligence, and dealing with your real estate investments. As you start building your real estate portfolio, having a reputable team can help you save a lot of time, resources, and money. The secret to building a successful team is to find reliable people to depend on. Build a reliable team of experts that you trust.

What Is the Purpose of this Team?

A complete team for your real estate business guide requires mentioning the value of building a successful real estate team. Each person has different real estate goals and ambitions, but no matter what yours are, you stand a better chance of attaining them with the help of your core team members. You must see your real estate investing team members as business partners that are important to helping you attain greater success in your real estate investing endeavour.

Who Are the Main Members of a Real Estate Investing Team?

Here are the members that make a great team. Let's look at each of them to better understand their role and purposes.

1. Spouse or Significant Other

Your spouse or that special someone plays a significant role in the success of your real estate investing journey. Having someone who you know will be on the same page with you all the time can help you emotionally in keeping yourself on track. The main reason as to why you need someone who is always on the same page with you is that this person has a big impact on life, and this person impacts the way you manage your funds, make your decisions, and work on your thoughts and ambitions.

2. Real Estate Agents

A real estate agent is another key member that will make your team strong and efficient. A reliable real estate agent can help you find the best deals available and put a bid on your behalf. He is familiar with the marketplace and knows how to do transactions. Real estate agents are able to act on behalf of the seller or buyer. Usually, real estate agents earn money by commission by the seller of a property. So, if you're thinking about adding a real estate agent to be in your team to help you purchase a property, this is going to be free. However, you have to make sure that you're not working with just any real estate agent. As much as possible, look for someone who really knows a thing or two about investing and has experience about it.

3. LENDERS

Forming strong relationships with conventional and private money lenders is a smart move for any real estate investor. Lenders could range from small community banks to credit unions to bigger commercial banks. Mortgage brokers and mortgage firms are also smart options. If those options are not enough, you can go with private or hard money lenders. No matter which path you decide to take on or when you choose to take it, the important thing is to build relationships with different lenders. Start to build relationships with these lenders now, so once a good opportunity comes, and it will, you will be ready with the right financing.

4. Contractors and Handymen

Having contractors and handymen in your team to deal with repairs is important for your real estate business. In order to find these people, you may ask for referrals from other real estate investors, or you can also find them online. Don't forget to check their references. Ask the contractor's references if they showed up on schedule and finished the work on time. Are they trustworthy? Did they do the job well? Are they trustworthy? Furthermore, you have to remember that the cheapest option may not be the best option. It might take some deep searching to find the perfect contractor, so being patient is important. You have to keep in mind that your goal is to build a team that can truly help you with your business.

5. Bookkeeper

You might want to have a bookkeeper in your team to help keep a good and accurate record of outgoing debits and incoming credits in the company. A bookkeeper could help you track all the expenses and income you can, and help prepare your finances throughout the tax season. An accurate account of income and expenses is important, and as you begin to generate more wealth and have more properties to manage, a reliable bookkeeper can be really beneficial for your business.

6. Accountant

Having a certified public accountant or CPA to your real estate team is also a very smart decision. A CPA can take the responsibility of preparing your personal and business tax returns, and on top of that, you can offer you solid advice when it comes to tax recommendations. Search for an accountant who has worked with other real estate experts or who knows a lot about real estate. Search for this team member as soon as possible, since a good CPA could help you pick the best tax-saving strategy for real estate investment.

7. Lawyer

A lawyer is an important part of any real estate team. A good lawyer can help draft and perform legally binding leases as well as other real estate documentation. Try to search for a lawyer that knows real estate or has worked with real estate investors in the past. A real estate lawyer could help you choose and set up the best legal article for managing your real estate properties.

8. Property Manager

The last but definitely not least is a property manager. From screening the tenants to making sure everything in order in the property itself, a property manager can help relieve you from some of the most time consuming and arduous tasks. This is something you want to look for once you have a fair amount of cash flow coming in and want your empire running as passive as it possibly can be. Do a thorough search in order to find a great property manager, and remember to check references.

WHEN SHOULD YOU BUILD YOUR REAL ESTATE INVESTING TEAM?

You must start your real estate investing team as soon as you can. The value your team increases as you make your professional relationship. These people are your teammates, and being aware of these key individuals as early as possible can help you attain success faster. Your real estate team could help throughout the due diligence period before even buying the property.

Chapter 12

SCALING YOUR REAL ESTATE EMPIRE

For many investors, closing a couple of deals automatically means success. Maybe they've found a couple of great units and started getting them rented out. Or maybe you could add a house a year to your rental properties. But still, after starting off well on your business, it might still hit a plateau. And the fundamental difference between growing and scaling a business is one of the main reasons as to why this is the case.

The skills needed to grow a business and how to scale it actually vary. Your ability to grow your business usually depends just on your hustle and knowledge. In terms of scaling a business, it is a whole different ballpark.

With scaling, you're creating a foundation that gives you a room to grow and develop your business in future. If your goal is to expand your business by 100%, then you must prepare yourself to give your 100% as well. It always seems like 24 hours in a day are not enough for you to do everything you need to do. One of the best things to do is to search for ways how you can grow your small business into a big one by working smarter rather than working harder.

And to scale your real estate investment business properly, here are some methods you can follow.

- **Choose a niche**

"Shiny object syndrome" is a common condition that many entrepreneurs acquire. When you start mastering something, there is a chance a tendency for it to be quite a boring routine. As a businessman, this is something you need to avoid.

And to successfully evade this situation, there are three things you have to answer when you're in the business of real estate investment – or just about any kind of business.

The questions are:

- ❖ What's your passion?

- ❖ What can your organization do that is better than the competition?

- ❖ How good it is when it comes to generating revenue?

Once you have answered this question, find out the most relevant niche to the set of answers you come up with.

You can't find a lot of market segments like this for most companies. Keep in mind that it's hard to focus on different types of the market at the same time – it's possible but almost unbearable. For example, if your company focuses on buying and flipping real estate in working to middle-class areas, it's not going be very smart to get involved with low-income housing or luxury housing without making a very well-organized plan. If you can scale your business, it's going to be easy for you to focus! You may be familiar with different types of real estate investments, but don't expect to be an expert on any of them.

- **Create a Brain Trust**

In running a business, and searching for the right team to help you, the secret is to find and hire people that are smarter than you. It doesn't matter how smart you are; being good at everything is just too draining. This might involve requiring finding partners, searching for mentors, or forming a "mastermind group," but it's very important to search for people who can do everything you can and more.

Of course, putting it on the backburner is very easy, but you have to make a point to prioritize it as a part of the routine. And you will want to have more people to help you with your venture as your business expands.

- **Delegate**

As stated above, working harder is not enough to make your business work and grow. We only have 24 hours in a day, and they are not enough for everything we want and need to do. So, in order for you to manage your tasks better, you must learn how to delegate.

Economists have this term called "opportunity cost", which refers to when an investor or business misses out on something when picking out one alternative over another. In other words, when you're doing one thing at the moment, it means you're missing out something else. Always remember that time is money, so you have to make the most of it. And the best way to do that is to learn how to delegate.

Before hiring a single employee, you are able to delegate tasks to realtors, accountants, lawyer, property managers, and anyone on your team. You can even hire an assistant to help you do simple tasks for you that even though you know you can do yourself, it is much better if you do something else more profitable and beneficial for you in the long run. And automating as many things as possible becomes easier. And once you know that you're ready, you can delegate more tasks and responsibilities to more employees.

Doing this thing will help you free up your time and get the money faster. The delegation also offers what we have known as "intrinsic motivation" to the employees. Having sovereignty is a real motivator for people while being controlled can sap the motivation of any.

- **Trust, but verify**

Of course, with delegation comes a catch. You can always guarantee for people you delegate to actually do the job that is assigned to them. Realtors, assistants, contractors, and just about anyone else can also waste your money without giving you something valuable to your organization.

But there's something you can do to prevent this, which is to *measure*. Measuring, however, doesn't only go for more than only the performance of the employee. For all rehabs, make sure to always compare the actual expenses to the budget, even though it didn't go well and looking at it can be quite scary. By not looking at it carefully, you wouldn't know what's wrong, and you wouldn't know how to improve it.

For any of your employees, you must strive to make KPI or Key Performance Indicators. Every employee must be assigned to do specific tasks and cover a certain area of focus. And there has to key numbers that will measure their performance. Always take proper precautions on this, though. A real estate agent who just does most of the most complicated tasks might find it hard to finish all the tasks he needed to do. That's why it's a good idea to have some KPIs for all the positions and watch out for the confounding factors.

- **Standardize**

Figure out what renovations are going to add the most value to your investment properties derived from the return on investment, property type, comps, location, as well as other factors. Then, you may want to apply the same set of rehabilitations on each of the properties. For example, if your company uses the same interior paint, furniture, carpet, and blinds most of the rental units or units you sell, you may want to use a different colour, but use the same brand. You can stick to several colours and may switch up every so often, but as much as possible, you may want to use standardized brands.

All in all, scaling a business is deeper than how it can be seen from the outside. Keep in mind that these processes will let you grow your real estate business quicker than you could have possibly imagined, and you can do it easier as well. Similar to a house, a business couldn't be built without foundation.

12.1 Most Cost-Effective Strategies and Ways to Grow Your Businesses

The real estate market has been extremely robust, giving a lot of investors a great opportunity to increase sales transactions and earn a lot more income than they did many years ago.

Of course, there's no denying that technology has played a huge role in this growth in the real estate market. If your goal is to master this craft or at least prepare yourself to easily adapt in the industry, here are some ways you can follow to your make your business successful and make it grow.

1. Invest for appreciation

Improving investment properties with predictable appreciation down the line in order to generate better returns is the best strategy to develop a business. However, you must keep in mind that putting an investment for appreciation is a long-term approach doesn't guarantee that you will get good cash flow returns right away. But many smart investors choose to invest exclusively for appreciation. These people see the financial rewards overtime contrasted with the immediate cash fixes ones who choose to go short term get. If you invest exclusively for appreciation, know that this is riskier compared to investing for cash flow, but the ROI is much better.

2. Maximize positive cash flow properties

One of the best strategies you can follow to grow your business is to find positive cash flow properties. In other words, positive cash flow properties reap investors an excess of cash returns and cover the costs of owning the property altogether.

3. Utilize home equity to purchase more real estate

Another smart approach that we have previously mentioned in this book is to jumpstart your real estate investing through your home equity. If you're in a financial restraint, you may want to consider the use of your home equity as leverage to purchase real estate. This method will also save you money, and it doesn't require you to lean down backwards to pay the deposit straight from your own pocket.

4. Expand your real estate portfolio

Expanding is something you may learn to do. This is because by doing this, you increase your returns and at the same time, minimalizing the overall risk. If you want to be successful in this, you must learn how to expand

and seek profitable real estate opportunities the best you can.

5. Renovate the property for maximum economic benefits

Renovation or home improvement, as mentioned in the earlier part of this book, is an important thing to do if you want to increase the value of the property, may it be for rental or selling purpose. The advice I want to give you is to learn how to recognize and prioritize work in the property that will provide you with the most benefits. This means you don't have to do renovations on it all at the same time. Instead, choose an area you think will be noticed by the potential buyer or tenant right away and fix it, then worry about the other parts later on.

6. Assign a Property Manager if needed

If managing daily operation has become overwhelming for you, then it's going to make more sense to get help from a professional who will be more than willing to help you run your business and keep your costs to a minimum. Hiring good property management can help you get a better ROI. This is especially the case if you have invested in multiple real estate properties.

All in all, being successful in this business involves business planning. This will help you maximize returns and giving you a business that will you lead you to financial freedom. Plan well and choose the best real estate growth strategy alongside your visions and financial objectives. Keep in mind that most successful real estate investors started off small and eventually worked their way up to win big.

Conclusion

Real estate offers many investment opportunities to anyone who is willing to try it. Generally, a lot of money might be required to get into this kind of business. Building your cash savings and reserves is necessary. While you're unlikely to risk your whole life savings if you make an investment in this field, but it's important to educate yourself. The return goes up in time and doesn't diminish if you know how to invest wisely.

As you can tell from this book, investing in real estate is one of the most complicated business activities you can do, but at the same time, it is rewarding in the long run. The truth is, this is a renowned investment vehicle particularly for the middle and upper class. Most people who have tried investing in real-estate have found this extremely rewarding even though it involves a lot of risks and effort.

Investing in this business is something that you must think about very carefully. Don't just get yourself into it unless you're 100% sure that you can handle it. But no matter how complicated it may seem, remember that this is something that anyone can learn with a great amount of dedication.

You must be aware that if you are new to this, you may face a lot of surprises, especially in the first part, which is the purchasing of the property. At first, you must determine what type of property investment you want to make before even looking for a house. Some of the most common investment property sources that you might consider include real estate agents, foreclosure sales, multiple listing services, and private sales.

You can find different ways to earn money from real estate you invested in. You might have it rented or appreciate its value by building equity. These are types of investments that can appreciate in value, and the property could provide you with an amazing increase in earnings after some years if done well. While real estate can generate long term income, as an investor, you must ask for advice from an experienced person or an expert who you know can develop and deliver an effective strategy from experience.

www.ingramcontent.com/pod-product-compliance
Lightning Source LLC
Chambersburg PA
CBHW030512210326

41597CB00013B/882